ROSAMOND LEHMANN IN VEGAS

ROSAMOND LEHMANN IN VEGAS

A COLLECTION OF RIOTOUSLY
ENTERTAINING COLUMNS,
WRITTEN FOR *THE BELIEVER*
MAGAZINE DURING ITS YEARS
IN THE DESERT

BELIEVER BOOKS
a division of
MCSWEENEY'S

BELIEVER BOOKS

a division of
MCSWEENEY'S

849 Valencia Street
San Francisco, CA 94110

These pieces appeared between September 2017 and
December 2021 in *The Believer* magazine.

www.thebeliever.net

ISBN: 978-1-95211-998-9

ALSO BY NICK HORNBY

Fiction
Just Like You
State of the Union
Funny Girl
Juliet, Naked
Slam
A Long Way Down
How to Be Good
About a Boy
High Fidelity

Nonfiction
Dickens and Prince: A Particular Kind of Genius
More Baths Less Talking
Shakespeare Wrote for Money
Housekeeping vs. the Dirt
The Polysyllabic Spree
Songbook
Fever Pitch

Anthology
Speaking with the Angel

Screenplay
An Education

CONTENTS

INTRODUCTION
by CLAIRE DEDERER

I write this in the fall of 2023. I mention the date because we've been living through a truly rotten period in history. I won't go into my personal litany of woes, on account of *who cares*. My little difficulties, and yours, nest inside the larger difficulties of the world—an absolutely undesired and unwelcome global communion. In the midst of all this, I experienced a feeling of inadequacy shared by many. I thought: What should I *do*? How should I meet this terrible moment?

Well, one way I met this terrible moment was by keeping a Google Doc listing all the books I read. I admit it's not exactly heroic—I didn't even turn my list into a charming monthly column. (I'm just a person, not a goddamn superhero!) But I found that logging my reading spurred me to read more books, and reading more books kept me out of trouble—the kind of trouble that happens inside a person, the kind of trouble she inflicts on herself. I could say something here about how in dark times, art is vital, blah, blah, blah... but I'm really talking here about sheer *volume*. Logging books kept me reading, reading more books kept me happier—it's as simple as that.

I know what Nick Hornby's "Stuff I've Been Reading" column does for us, his readers: it provides us with a seemingly endless supply of brilliant, witty essays that somehow manage to be both generous and deliciously crotchety. But based on my own experience with tracking my reading, I began to wonder: What are these columns doing for Nick Hornby? Is it possible that documenting his monthly consumption has kept him reading, and therefore kept him happy? I find this a comforting thought. A happy and healthy Nick Hornby is good for all of us. Or maybe that is too pious a thought. Maybe I don't really care if Nick Hornby is happy and healthy, except in a kind of pro forma

"May all beings be well" kind of way. Maybe I only really care if Nick Hornby is productive.

Productivity. It's a chilly-sounding word that denotes a hot reality: we want more, more, more from the artists we love; we want them never to stop making things for us to consume. This sentiment is echoed by... hold on a second: What to call him? Hornby? Nick? The former feels a little too starchy, too *Herr Professor*, for the author of the "Stuff I've Been Reading" column, which slings an arm over its readers' shoulders and leans in conspiratorially to say what it has to say. The latter is impertinent. I suppose we'll have to keep calling him Nick Hornby. Anyway, this sentiment is echoed by Nick Hornby himself, who writes in a column collected here about how he also yearns for productivity from his favorite writers: "I don't want anyone to stop, really. I want Casey Cep and Jessica Chiccehitto Hindman, neither of whom has written books before, to take the Mike Nichols path through life rather than the [Harper] Lee route." (He's referring here to Mike Nichols's fabulous decades of, yes, productivity, as opposed to Harper Lee's disappearing act.) He goes on: "I hope they write tons more books, and that these books become brilliant Oscar-winning films, with fantastic soundtracks (none of which feature a penny whistle). We need as much good stuff as people can make. I never want to stop consuming it, that's for sure."

This volume marks twenty years since Nick Hornby started writing the column for *The Believer*. Like many of you, I've been with him all along. It would be pleasingly Hornby-esque to describe in detail the hours I've spent happily reading his descriptions of happily reading someone else. Put it this way: I read *Ten Years in the Tub* in the tub. My reading of Nick Hornby's reading has been a doubling that is one of the best loneliness mitigators I know of. I read him reading, and my own responses are reflected back to me, except, you know, *smart*. The columns are almost miraculous in the way they use voice, bringing the reader closer and closer; they're little intimacy factories. As I made my way through this collection, I started thinking about how these columns—along with Nick Hornby's novels, essays, film and television scripts, and on and on—have kept me company over the last decades. I never want to stop consuming his work, and I've never had to.

I allowed myself to wonder, for a dizzying moment: What if he stopped? And I didn't care for that idea one bit. A world without Nick Hornby? It must come one day, but not yet, please. I feel a bit like a spouse in one of those very long marriages, hoping I will die before he does so I won't have to miss him, and by him I mean Nick Hornby, provider of good things to read. This paragraph has gotten much darker than I intended.

I began this little introduction in darkness, and that's where I've ended up. That's where Nick Hornby ends up, too, in a column dated a year and a half into the pandemic. The final paragraph reads: "It's the end of the English summer. It rained, mostly. But these were the books that made the wet and the cold bearable. When the sun eventually did come out, and I found myself reading Elizabeth Strout on a sun lounger by a pond, the brightness and warmth seemed almost de trop. We have all learned something like that these last eighteen months: that the outside world doesn't matter so much if we allow talented people to cast their light when we need it." To call Nick Hornby talented is a massive understatement—like saying LeBron is pretty sporty. The light he casts is a durable consolation for the darkness of the world. I for one would like it never to go out. ✶

OCTOBER/NOVEMBER 2017

BOOKS READ:

- ★ *Topless Cellist: The Improbable Life of Charlotte Moorman*—Joan Rothfuss
- ★ *Contested Will: Who Wrote Shakespeare?*—James Shapiro
- ★ *The Awkward Age*—Francesca Segal
- ★ *A Horse Walks Into a Bar*—David Grossman

BOOKS BOUGHT:

- ★ *The Tidal Zone*—Sarah Moss
- ★ *The Origins of Cool in Postwar America*—Joel Dinerstein
- ★ *The Story of a Brief Marriage*—Anuk Arudpragasam
- ★ *Once*—Meghan O'Rourke
- ★ *Suite for Barbara Loden*—Nathalie Léger
- ★ *Mother of Sorrows*—Richard McCann

The story so far: the Polysyllabic Spree, the ninety-seven young, elegant, cultured, aromatic, but occasionally gullible editors of *The Believer*, went to Vegas, got drunk, and put everything they owned—namely, this magazine, plus some aromatherapy oil and a couple of chapbooks—on the number 21 in a game of roulette. They lost, and a dubious but so far perfectly amiable group of gangsters called the Black Mountain Mob now oversee these pages. I am writing in isolation here in London, and can only presume that by the time you see it, this column will be surrounded by advertisements for fire-arms and articles about how to design authentic-looking designer labels for bootleg whiskey, but no matter! The BMM has assured me that they are still very interested in the stuff I've been reading, and I will take them at their word. They were particularly excited by Joan Rothfuss's *Topless Cellist*, which they thought promised the kind of cross-promotional synergy they were looking for. I haven't yet dared confess what it's about, because what it's about is some of the more outré artistic experiments of the 1960s and '70s, although some of them do involve nudity.

During the Fourth Annual New York Avant Garde Festival in Central Park, on September 9, 1966, the following pieces were performed: Yoko Ono's *Sunrise Event*, in which the audience watched the sun come up; Kurt Schwitters's *Class Struggle Opera*, in which the cast, some of whom were perched on a stepladder, shouted "up" and "down" at one another; Nam June Paik's *Zen Smiles*, in which five thousand pennies were handed out to anyone who wanted them; Wolf Vostell's *Morning Glory*, in which *The New York Times* was sprinkled with pepper and perfume and then whizzed up in a blender (the resulting paste was then buried in a flower garden while sneeze powder was chucked about in the air with gay abandon); Giuseppe Chiari's *Fuori (Outdoors)*, wherein a performer sat on a floating stage in a pond and listened to the sounds around her; and, perhaps most notably, especially for those who caught it, Jim McWilliams's *American Picnic*, in which McWilliams and a protégé ate hot dogs and water-melons, washed the food down with soda, and puked it all up again.

I love reading about the avant-garde, not least because these pieces, it seems to me, are best enjoyed in books. Even the slowest reader can enjoy them in just a few seconds, whereas experiencing many of them live, in the flesh (and there was a lot of flesh around), would have taken several hours—hours which, it is fair to say, were not without their longueurs. Rothfuss's gripping biography of Charlotte Moorman contains dizzying, frequently hilarious accounts of many, frankly insane, artistic experiments; on more or less every page, I was thinking, simultaneously, I'm so glad I know about this stuff, and, I'm so glad I didn't have to sit through any of it. Charlotte Moorman and her partner, Nam June Paik, the Korean artist of penny-dispensing fame, devised a program entitled *As Boring as Possible*, a performance of which would typically last five hours, although—presumably emboldened by their success—the duo later staged an expanded version. In 1959, Rothfuss tells us, Paik had "defined his action-music strategies as 'constant surprise, disappointment, and extreme tedium,'" and there is plenty of evidence in this book that he triumphed over and over again.

Charlotte Moorman was a classically trained cellist from Little Rock, Arkansas, who showed little sign, in her youth, of turning into the kind of woman who would, in 1967, find herself in court facing charges of indecent exposure. The very first show she helped produce, for the Japanese violinist Kenji Kobayashi, necessitated the pouring of tiny plastic beads over piano strings in order to make a lovely tinkly noise. This, presumably, produced a few seconds of pleasure for the members of the audience; it also created a hell of a clearing-up job, and Moorman and Kobayashi were up all night picking beads out of the piano with damp cotton-buds. Welcome to the avant-garde.

The nudity came later, during her partnership with Paik, who was of the view that a "historical blunder" had kept sex out of classical music. He and Moorman spent a good chunk of their time attempting to correct the mistake, mostly by playing without clothes on. I am not sure their heroic efforts paid off, long-term. Classical music still isn't as sexy as it might be. Or am I missing something? The weird thing about histories of the avant-garde is that you start to doubt the "avant." The "garde" are those of us trudging along behind the visionaries and experimenters, right? But doesn't that mean we should eventually reach the territory they have already left behind? Shouldn't we be looking back at these bold 1960s experiments and thinking, Huh. I always wondered who started that whole art-puking thing that everyone does nowadays? Perhaps *dehors*—outside—might be a better preposition then *avant*. If we in the garde still haven't got with the program, then these guys aren't avant anything.

I am a sucker for buying books from galleries after exhibitions, and these purchases almost always turn out to be the result of temporary enthusiasms. I walk out of the gallery and into the gift shop with the intention of reading everything there is to read on the exhibition's subject, an intention that frequently vanishes at some point during the Tube ride home. Looking at the hundreds of unread books on my shelves, I can see a Penguin collection of artists' manifestos, and a book about Lenin that came from a Soviet exhibition at the British Library, and a book about Cinecittà that dates from a photography show about *La dolce vita*. Only *Topless Cellist* has made it through to the top of the reading pile. It would be pathetic if the title alone were responsible for my commitment, but if the book had been called *Charlotte Moorman: Dadaist Provocateur*, I don't suppose I would have picked it up. (Moorman was dubbed "the Topless Cellist" by the tabloids after her court case—a "ludicrous and reductive" nickname, as Rothfuss points out, although she seemed to find it useful for her book.) I'm glad I did bite, though. Joan Rothfuss is an exemplary biographer: concise, sympathetic, skeptical in all the right places, and an engaging storyteller. I was surprised frequently, but never disappointed or bored.

The modern age does not have a monopoly on eccentric thinking about the arts, and James Shapiro's *Contested Will: Who Wrote Shakespeare?* is in parts just as funny as *Topless Cellist*. The refusal to believe that William Shakespeare wrote the plays and poems of William Shakespeare has been going on for over two hundred years now, and shows no signs of dying down: a one-star review of Shapiro's book on Amazon by an angry reader describes it as "a waste of space and effort," and the reviewer has awarded one- or two-star reviews to another dozen or so books—by Shapiro, Stephen Greenblatt, Peter Ackroyd—that refuse to acknowledge that the Bard was actually somebody else entirely. The anti-Stratfordians (that's what they call themselves) aren't going away anytime soon.

They are a surprisingly starry bunch. Helen Keller and Mark Twain bonded over their belief that Shakespeare was in reality Francis Bacon. Orson Welles, Henry James, and Charlie Chaplin were anti-Stratfordians, too. Their odd and, one might argue, somewhat pointless beliefs stem either from snobbery (how could a provincial like Shakespeare have known about kings and courts and the like?) or from a simple conviction that, as all writing is essentially autobiographical, we have to look for a candidate whose experience most closely matches the experiences fictionalized in the plays. Meanwhile, Sigmund Freud's skepticism comes from somewhere else entirely. While working on his theories about the Oedipus complex, he became convinced that *Hamlet* was written while Shakespeare was grieving his father's death. He wasn't worried about whether Shakespeare was who he said he was, as it were, until years later, when scholarship dated *Hamlet* to a time *before* the playwright lost his father. At this point, Freud, so committed to the idea of Hamlet as a walking and talking—if entirely fictional—exemplar of an Oedipal fixation, decided it would be much easier to rewrite history than to rewrite his ideas, and became a devout Oxfordian. You've got to admire his nerve. Poor old Mark Twain became quite befuddled by Baconianism. He wrote a book entitled *Is Shakespeare Dead?*, great chunks of which were plagiarized, and came to believe that Queen Elizabeth must have been a man.

You can see the appeal of anti-Stratfordianism. It involves an awful lot of larky detective work—there were plenty of codes to be cracked and acrostics to find. A wealthy physician from Detroit, Orville W. Owen, went above and beyond the call of duty: he built a decoding machine, now owned, unpredictably, by Summit University, a Christian college in Montana. The machine was foolproof. Two large drums, on which revolved a two-foot-wide and thousand-foot-long canvas sheet, on which one pasted not just the works of Bacon and Shakespeare but the works of all Bacon's other pseudonyms, most notably Marlowe, Spenser, and Robert Burton. You turned the wheel a couple of times, key words would reveal themselves, and bingo! You could prove anything you wanted to. Owen got a six-volume book out of it, *Sir Francis Bacon's Cipher Story*. Please forgive me, dear reader, when I tell you that I haven't even looked at it.

This is the third of Shapiro's books about Shakespeare that I've read, after *A Year in the Life of William Shakespeare: 1599* and *The Year of Lear: Shakespeare in 1606*. All three of them are gripping, learned, and quite frequently instructive about things only incidentally connected to Shakespeare. *Contested Will* is about the crankiness of literary scholars, snobbery, self-delusion, and the modernity of autobiography. Enough to be going on with? I should hope so.

Nobody in Francesca Segal's lovely, elegant, soulful novel *The Awkward Age* is mad, as such, but two of the characters are maddening, mostly because they are teenagers. I have two teenage boys in my house, and I can no longer remember the last time they made a decision that a rational child would have reached, let alone a rational adult. (If you think I'm being cruel, be assured that they will never read these words, because, you know… reading.) *The Awkward Age* is about a new family, formed when a widowed woman falls in love with a divorcé. To begin with, there is only friction, because the woman's teenage daughter and the man's teenage son can't stand each other. But eventually the hormones kick in, and stepbrother and stepsister start getting it on, at which point all domestic hell breaks loose. It's a brilliant, high-concept story that is at the same time a literary novel—another way of saying, I suppose, that this novel is as many more novels should be: readable, careful, thoroughly imagined, surprising.

Segal's first novel, *The Innocents*, drew comparisons to Monica Ali and Zadie Smith, mostly because (a) Segal is a woman and (b) she is Jewish, and her novels contain observations about Jewishness. And yes, I know Monica Ali was born in Bangladesh and Zadie Smith is half-Jamaican, *but that is how some English literary critics think*: these writers are bringing us News from Elsewhere, even though all three of them are writing about their own, entirely native versions of London. *The Innocents* was a terrific first novel but *The Awkward Age* is a step up. The stakes are higher, the minor characters are superbly imagined, and the end is completely satisfying, even though it doesn't go…

Actually, scrap the "even though." Never mind how or where it doesn't go. I want you to read it.

David Grossman's *A Horse Walks Into a Bar*, winner of this year's Man Booker International Prize, is every bit as gripping as Segal's novel, with one crucial difference: if you read it in a hot place, you will need to wrap a towel around yourself, and you will need cold water near at hand. I just re-read that sentence, and I might inadvertently have given the impression that we're back in *Topless Cellist* territory, but it's not that at all: set entirely over the course of an evening, it's about a stand-up comedian's nervous breakdown during a show, and the sweat Grossman induces comes from excruciation. It's an extraordinary book, best read quickly for full effect (it's short, so it feels roughly the length of the comedian's set): it moves like a train, and crushes everyone in its path. In the audience are two people who know the comedian from his childhood days, and one of these two is the narrator of the novel. As the set builds to a climax, with a long, terrible story about a childhood trauma, the narrator realizes he is implicated. There are even a couple of good jokes in the novel, although it's fair to say it's not a funny book. Rather, it's in the great tradition of prize-winning fiction, which means you're left with the feeling of wanting to hang yourself. But in a good way.

So there we are. The end of my first column for my new editor, who goes by the street name of the Bloody Pencil. I'm trying not to read anything into it. If I fail to reappear, you will know that our literary tastes are not convergent. And you may have to dredge the Thames. ✷

DECEMBER 2017/JANUARY 2018

BOOKS READ:

* *Lonesome Dove*—Larry McMurtry
* *The Trip to Echo Spring: On Writers and Drinking*—Olivia Laing
* *Satan Is Real: The Ballad of the Louvin Brothers*—Charlie Louvin with Benjamin Whitmer
* *"High Noon": The Hollywood Blacklist and the Making of an American Classic*—Glenn Frankel

BOOKS BOUGHT:

* *Less*—Andrew Sean Greer
* *Up the Down Staircase*—Bel Kaufman
* *A Life of My Own*—Claire Tomalin
* *Fall on Your Knees*—Ann-Marie MacDonald

So, where to start? With Olivia Laing's brilliant book about writers and booze, *The Trip to Echo Spring*? Glenn Frankel's scholarly, frightening *High Noon*, about the bitterly divisive making of the Gary Cooper movie during a very difficult period in America's cultural and political history? *Satan Is Real*, Charlie Louvin's startling history of his life in country music? Or *Lonesome Dove*, Larry McMurtry's 843-page novel about cattle, cowboys, Indians, whores, guns, life, death, the American West, and quite a few other chunks of the USA, and just about anything else you can think of, apart from Brexit and iPhones?

There's no contest, really. I loved everything I read this month, but the sheer scale of *Lonesome Dove* crushed everything in its path, including, in my case, not one but two family holidays. One always hopes to be transported somewhere else by a novel, even if the world depicted is only up the end of your street: it's still a world populated by the novelist's imagination, with a geography that has been mapped out by someone with a different vantage point from your own. I don't know, obviously, what it would feel like to read McMurtry's magnificent epic if you were an American; perhaps if you live in New York City or LA or in a suburb of Cleveland, surrounded by Starbucks and concrete, it might not seem so very different. I am an Englishman who set off on the novel's journey from Texas next to a swimming pool in France, and arrived in Montana while sitting by a pond in Dorset (another swimming pool, actually, albeit one designed to look like a pond, but I didn't want to repeat the words *swimming pool*, for various reasons). And I can say only that I was transported somewhere else so completely that if I'd had to shoot a couple of children in order to get my lunch, I would have done so, without really thinking about it. Hour after hour after hour, I was taken to places I had never really thought about, or at least not since I was very young, and I became lost in them.

Lonesome Dove is the story of a cattle drive, and if you're all like, *No, I don't want to read about a cattle drive. I want to read about 1970s campus adultery*, I would ask you to rethink your position, because the first thing to say about *Lonesome Dove* is that there are enormous narrative events on a regular basis. People are killed by snakes. There are sandstorms. There are bad men who shoot people, then hang them, then burn them, mostly for the hell of it. It's all a bit of a shock to the system, if your normal literary diet consists of the sort of novel in which a narrator spends thirty years thinking about something enigmatic that happened to him in his teens. I read these books, too, and while chomping through *Lonesome Dove*, I spent half the time wondering whether one was allowed to write about snakes and dismemberment in literary fiction. Isn't it too easy, describing a landscape and a time in which shit not only happens, but never stops happening? Doesn't the real skill of the contemporary novelist's craft lie in our ability to bang on for fifty pages about interiors—not just wallpaper and furniture, but the psyche and the state of the soul?

The price that McMurtry has to pay for this kind of cheating, surely, is that he loses everything that proper literary fiction, the ruminative kind, does so well: characterization, deft shifts of tone, depth, heart, humor, empathy, pain. Inexplicably, they are all there. I regret to inform you that the characters are unforgettable, that *Lonesome Dove* is properly funny, and that it will both stop and break your heart. OK, the sentences are not Jamesian. But Jamesian sentences would be as much use out on the trail as an ice cream maker, and in any case McMurtry's sentences are sturdily built. And some of the minor characters are Dickensian, an adjective that's unavoidable in describing a novel as rich, as teeming with life, and as ambitious as this one. Deets and July Johnson, Lori and Elmira, Frog Lip and Blue Duck, Jake Spoon and Dish Boggett... There are scores of people in this book, all lovingly delineated, most of them complicated, all of them existentially tough, damaged by the lives they have had to live. It's not even as if the narrative goes in a straight line, even though a straight line would plot the course that most of the characters take. There are subplots, characters peel off and settle somewhere along the trail, traumatized and brutalized by their experiences along the way. And there are deaths, of course, all of them violent, some of them startlingly so. They are not random, in the sense that there is a rhythm to them, and the saddest death is saved for last. (If you intend to read the book, don't make the mistake I made, which was to search online for a map of the route. The first thing I saw was the location of the grave of... Well, never mind whose grave it was. But learning that he was dead was devastating in several ways: I was overwhelmed by grief, because I loved him, and I was extremely upset that I had to root for him over hundreds of pages with the unwanted knowledge that my support and concern were going to prove fruitless.)

Lonesome Dove is a major American novel, and yet it's proving to be a hard sell, especially to British women. There are female characters in this book, and they are drawn with love and sympathy, but they are pretty much all either whores or wives, frequently both, with the first calling preceding the second. One of them is raped repeatedly, after being abducted, and she is rendered almost mute by the experience;

McMurtry treats her painfully slow recovery with suitable weight and sobriety. But there simply isn't an awful lot of leaning in to be done, and if it's any consolation, the lives of the men are just as cheap.

But part of the resistance I am meeting is that *Lonesome Dove* is a cowboy book: John Wayne, Roy Rogers and Trigger, Bonanza, B movies, and 1930s serials—none of which have survived to compete with, say, Louis Armstrong or Buster Keaton as serious pillars of early American pop culture— don't help my cause. Kids don't even pretend to be cowboys anymore, not round my way. But McMurtry begins with a quote from T. K. Whipple's *Study Out the Land*: "All America lies at the end of the wilderness road, and our past is not a dead past, but still lives in us. Our forefathers had civilization inside themselves, the wild outside. We live in the civilization they created, but within the US the wilderness still lingers. What they dreamed, we live, and what they lived, we dream." What better time to read this magnificent book than now, when America is once again trying to decide what it wants to dream, and what it wants to live?

In one of those magical reading moments that happen sometimes, I traveled with Augustus McCrae and W. F. Call from Texas to Montana, put down *Lonesome Dove* with a full and heavy heart, picked up *High Noon*, and read this, the first sentence of the first chapter: "In 1914, when Frank Cooper was thirteen years old, his father took him to the state capitol building in Helena, Montana, to see a stunning new mural created by Charles M. Russell, one of the great artist-mythmakers of the Old West." What are the odds? They are considerably shortened, I suppose, if you move from one book featuring a man in a cowboy hat on the front cover to another book featuring a man in a cowboy hat on the front cover. But even so! Spooky, no? Oh, suit yourself. *"High Noon": The Hollywood Blacklist and the Making of an American Classic* seems simultaneously timely and quaint—quaint because whatever else we're afraid of at the moment, communism no longer keeps us awake at night; timely because then, like now, the political climate was ugly, paranoid, and bitterly divisive.

The three central characters in Frankel's study are Frank (later Gary) Cooper, who changed his name to the Indiana town of his agent's birth; Carl Foreman, the screenwriter of the movie; and Stanley Kramer, the producer. Of the three, it was Foreman who suffered most from the blacklist: he was forced to move to England to work while *High Noon* was still in production, and ended up never really going home. Impressively, he ended up involved in some iconic British films, after writing an iconic piece of Americana: he was an uncredited writer on *The Bridge on the River Kwai*, David Lean's beloved epic, although his credit was eventually restored, and he was awarded a posthumous Oscar. (The Oscar was originally awarded to the author of the novel that the film is based on, Frenchman Pierre Boulle, who not only didn't write the screenplay but couldn't speak English.) (Oh, and Boulle's other major novel was—wait for it—*Planet of the Apes*.) (I'm sorry about all the parentheses, but when writing about books like this, full of delightful but thematically unconnected trivia, they are unavoidable.) It seems only right that *High Noon* is full of heroes and villains. John Wayne, the man who wouldn't fight the Nazis, was instrumental in driving Foreman out of Hollywood; Stanley Kramer, Foreman's friend and business partner, never spoke to him again after Foreman's use of the Fifth Amendment in front of the House Un-American Activities Committee, in order to avoid naming names. Gary Cooper, a staunch Republican and a deeply flawed husband, but a kind man, was human enough to try and help Foreman out, but Wayne and his bullying soon put a stop to that. *High Noon*, the screenwriter explained during his testimony, was "the story of a town that died because it lacked the moral fiber to withstand aggression." Perhaps the timeliness is much more significant than the quaintness.

I haven't read anyone quite like Olivia Laing. *The Trip to Echo Spring* is a work of literary criticism, I suppose, but it's also a travel book, and it contains fragments of memoir and potted biographies, but there's an ache to it, too, a deep sadness, which comes partly from the author's love for and helpless frustration with the writers she studies, but also simply because the book is about success and failure, life and death, parents and children, relationships and betrayals. And, yes, these were the subjects of the drunk writers she discusses here—Berryman, Carver, Tennessee Wiliams, Cheever, Hemingway, and Fitzgerald—but the affecting tone of Laing's book isn't arrived at vicariously, if you see what I mean. The damaged lives become the fabric of the author's own purposes, and *The Trip to Echo Spring* thus becomes, emphatically, a work of art, with a voice and a mood all its own. You learn things, of course. You learn not just about the books and plays and poems, the sometimes difficult conditions in which they were produced, but also about alcohol itself, what it does to people. Laing quotes a report on the impossible conundrums of alcoholism: "This hyperactivity in the brain produces an intense need to calm down and to use more alcohol," before remarking, wearily, "What a mess. What a bloody mess." It's a lovely, characteristic moment in a beautiful book.

The Louvin Brothers, or one of them, anyway, could hold their own in any book about the baleful effects of drink on a career. Ira Louvin was the problem, according to his brother Charlie's book about their career in country music. Drink cost Ira his career, a relationship with his brother, and several wives, but despite the chaos it engendered, it's dealt with matter-of-factly here: there are eye-widening accounts of fistfights and binges (poor old Charlie even gets clonked on the head with a skillet, rather like a country-music Homer Simpson), and of course Charlie regrets the ruinous path that his brother chose. But mostly this book is about what it was like to grow up dirt-poor, talented, and ambitious, and even though you may think there are no surprises left in this kind of story, Louvin's gleeful details are fresh and, sometimes, sad and funny at the same time. How do you listen to music late at night when your father is likely to give you a severe beating if he hears the record player being used? Charlie Louvin had the answer. You sneak downstairs, take a couple of broom straws, put them between your teeth, and use them as styli, and the music goes straight into your skull. The desperate artist's need for art will always find a way, however unpromising the circumstances.

Four books, all about the best that America has to offer: movies, vernacular music, writers who meant and continue to mean something the world over, an implacable landscape, and an extraordinary history. It occurred to me that I would happily read novels and biographies about America and Americans for the rest of my life, so important has the United States been to me both professionally and as a cultural consumer, but maybe it's time to turn my attention to my own benighted, lonely island. The summer is over now, America has gone mad anyway, and I am hoping that one of my countrymen can explain to me, in some form of writing, what the hell is going on here. It is somewhat startling to realize that if I were to embark on a two-thousand-mile cattle drive from London—and I haven't ruled it out completely—I'd end up somewhere near Marrakech if I went south, or near Moscow if I went east. That's a lot of paperwork, especially now that we have torn up all the livestock agreements with EEC countries. We don't have the room to dream in the same way as America does, which is why we need you to dream for us. Please don't stop. ✴

FEBRUARY/MARCH 2018

BOOKS READ:

* *Unleashing Demons: The Inside Story of Brexit*—Craig Oliver
* *A Life of My Own*—Claire Tomalin
* *The Lonely City*—Olivia Laing
* *The Party*—Elizabeth Day

BOOKS BOUGHT:

* *The Last Poets*—Christine Otten
* *Whatever Happened to Interracial Love?*—Kathleen Collins
* *To the River: A Journey Beneath the Surface*—Olivia Laing
* *The Book of Forgotten Authors*—Christopher Fowler
* *Trouble Boys: The True Story of the Replacements*—Bob Mehr
* *Vernon Subutex 1*—Virginie Despentes

A couple of weeks before the referendum in which the British people decided they no longer wanted to be part of the EU, I went to a literary festival in Stoke, a couple of hours north of London. Until that day, I had been working on the assumption that my countrymen would decide, without any great enthusiasm, not to rock the boat. Nobody loves the EU, but the chaos that threatened to engulf us if we chose to leave seemed real enough to deter risk. The time I spent in Stoke, however, taught me more than any amount of time spent reading *The Guardian*, listening to the BBC, and talking to my North London friends and colleagues, and what I learned was that there was real trouble brewing.

I was shown around Stoke by an enthusiastic local employer who loved the place, and had just moved there after years spent commuting to the city. Stoke, she pointed out, had once been a mining town, but the mines were now closed; it was also part of the region known as the Potteries (the local football team is nicknamed the Potters), but nearly all the potters had gone, too, mostly abroad. She was hopeful that better times were around the corner, and she told me about a scheme whereby anyone wanting to settle and work in the city could buy a house for a pound. American readers may be aware that there is a similar deal available in Detroit, and though it's an imaginative response to a terrible problem, it's not altogether good news, for obvious reasons. Later, I met the local Labour MP, who, unlike his leader, Jeremy Corbyn, was strongly committed to Europe. He told me glumly that he hadn't yet met a single resident who was going to vote Remain, and I started to feel prickles of alarm down the back of my neck. "What are you doing about it?" I asked him. "Well," he said, "at the moment I'm just not telling people there's a referendum on. That's about all I've got left."

Later on, I watched the TV news. We were being warned that a vote to leave would take thirty thousand pounds off the price of our houses, and several thousand pounds a year off our salaries. How must that have sounded to those who live in homes that are worth a pound, and who are working for minimum wage, if they're working at all? It almost certainly sounded as though none of it had anything to do with them. How can a house worth nothing lose thirty thousand pounds of its value? I turned the news off and placed a bet on Leave with an online bookmaker. The people of Stoke, it turned out, were more enthusiastic about leaving than people anywhere else in the country, but they weren't anomalous, and as you probably know, I won my bet. Michael Bloomberg recently said that "it is really hard to understand why a country that was doing so well wanted to ruin it," to which the only possible retort is that 51 percent of this country didn't share his rosy view of our economic prospects. The kind of wealth that the UK has been creating seems to take an awfully long time to trickle down to people without work, in areas of the country that have no industry.

Britain voted out because just enough people were angry with the status quo to want to change it, however disastrous that decision might prove to be in the short or even the long term. Give an angry, voiceless person a microphone, and the last thing they're going to say is *Actually, now that I come to think about it, let's just carry on the way we have been doing.* There seems little doubt to me that they voted against their economic interests; there seems even less doubt that they didn't care very much, because they felt they had no stake in the prosperity Bloomberg was talking about. (Americans may recognize this from some of their own recent electoral history.) Fears about immigration became more important than empty wallets—even though London, with its huge immigrant community, voted to stay in the EU by more or less exactly the same margin as Stoke voted to leave.

Unleashing Demons, written by David Cameron's former director of communications, Craig Oliver, is a fly-on-the wall account of the referendum campaign, and another version of why Britons voted out: not because of economics or immigration, but because of the way these concerns were presented to the electorate by the opposing campaigns. Written in diary form, it's a tragic book for those of us who were profoundly depressed by the result of the referendum: you know the unhappy ending in advance, and you can see the ways in which it might have been avoided. If only the Remain campaign hadn't won the economic argument so comprehensively and so early, thus ensuring that the last, decisive period before the vote was about immigration, the Remain campaign's weak spot. What Remain should have said is something like *Are you fucking kidding me? Every single hospital and care home in the country is staffed by European immigrants. Every single plumber is Polish. Every time you order takeaway, an immigrant delivers it. The whole reason the country hasn't fallen off a cliff is because we have immigration.* But of course nobody on the Remain side said that. They said, more or less, that they'd try and do something about it one day, and nobody believed them. If only the Labour Party had campaigned with even half a heart; if only Boris Johnson and Michael Gove, with one eye on succeeding David Cameron, hadn't told so many lies.

The diary format means that *Unleashing Demons* can't offer much perspective on the decisions and tactics, but the in-the-moment panics and stumbles provide plenty of fuel for hindsight. How could the prime minister fight a war against some of his own colleagues while trying to run the country? (He couldn't.) Why was Theresa May, Cameron's then home secretary and in theory a Remainer, playing it so cagey? (She was trying to become prime minister, and she didn't want to piss anyone off.) Why wouldn't Jeremy Corbyn, the leader of the Labour Party and in theory a Remainer, campaign with any kind of zeal? (Because he was trying to become prime minister, and he didn't want to piss anyone off.)

And Oliver raises all kinds of anguished and pertinent questions about fake news: How do neutral organizations like the BBC cover both sides of an argument fairly when one side is lying? The Leave campaign had a great time telling the people of Britain that they could save £350 million a week by getting out of the EU (they couldn't) and that seventy million Turks were on their way to the UK once Turkey joined the EC (which was never going to happen). The plodding one-side-says-this-but-the-other-side-says-that evenhandedness that the BBC (and *The New York Times*, and more or less every reputable media outlet) has relied on for so long seems out of step with the times. "People in this country have had enough of experts," said Michael Gove, former justice secretary and arch-Brexiteer, when he was asked during the campaign why no leading economists thought that leaving the EU was a good idea. It was a shocking moment: an Oxford-educated former leader and writer for *The Times* telling us that the facts don't matter. He was right, though, as it turned out. Michael Gove is now a pariah, the country is riven in two, our economy is going down the toilet, and it will take us decades to recover. Well done, everyone. I know you probably won't want to read this illuminating book, but I don't care. I wanted to find out what had happened, and I wanted to sound off. Let's move on.

"We grieved together over Brexit," says the literary biographer Claire Tomalin at the end of her wonderful memoir, *A Life of My Own*. The other half of the "we" is her husband, Michael Frayn, the brilliant playwright and novelist. They are both eighty-four years old, and more or less every single page of Tomalin's book makes you mourn the disappearance of an England that regarded an education as a source of liberation rather than mockery. In the only novel I read this month, Elizabeth Day's waspish, moreish *The Party*, the one educated and cultured character is a pathetic, somewhat creepy outsider, looking on with envy and contempt as his boorish school friends trample their way into positions of power and influence; that seems about right for now, for this version of Britain. And of course Tomalin's world of libraries, universities, publishers, and literary pages was available only to a very small number of people. But is it OK to love those people and wish they were still with us? I don't care if it is or isn't; I'm going to love them anyway. Tomalin was reading Dickens when she was little, French novels and the Brontës when she was ten, and she bought herself Eileen Power's *Medieval English Nunneries* when she was thirteen: "Power, a young woman historian, became my heroine." I'm sure she would have been mine, too, if TV hadn't been invented. And some other things (cinema, friends, music, et cetera). It's impossible to compare the intelligence of different generations, of course, but here at *The Believer* we tend to prize wide, deep reading as an indication of something, and there is absolutely no doubt that Tomalin's generation is better read than my own. And each subsequent generation after mine, I suspect, has read even less than the one before, until you get to... Actually, I'm not going to be rude about my sons again. But they won't be buying *Medieval English Nunneries* with their own money anytime soon.

None of this, I hasten to add, is about Tomalin showing off. In the early part of *A Life of My Own*, she's talking about reading as an escape, and of course the more you read, the farther you can run. Tomalin's childhood was not comfortable, financially or emotionally. Her father told her, inexplicably, that she was conceived on the day that he had seriously contemplated pushing her mother off a cliff during a walk. He left her, eventually, but he remained an occasionally unhelpful presence in his daughter's life: later, when Tomalin's first husband, Nick, left her, as he did on more than one occasion, for a younger woman, her father wrote to Nick to say, effectively, that living with women was hard, and that he couldn't blame him for clearing off.

Many of us who knew a little of what was going on in the world in the 1970s can remember Nick Tomalin, and the shock of his death: he was killed by a Syrian missile while covering the Yom Kippur War for *The Sunday Times*. And this happened during a ten-year period that contained more tragedy and challenge than most lives can properly accommodate. Her youngest son, Tom, conceived partly to plaster over the cracks of what had become a painful married life, was born with spina bifida; her daughter, Susanna, committed suicide. And yet *A Life of My Own* is not only about these awful things. They are deeply felt, and they explode like bombs; but then Tomalin goes on, changed forever, but with the rest of her life to live. Regular readers will know that I am an enormous admirer of the author's literary biographies. *The Invisible Woman*, about Dickens's relationship with the actress Nelly Ternan, is one of my favorite books of any type, and Tomalin's biographies of Hardy and Dickens are definitive. This book is as patient, as illuminating, and as acute as the rest of her work. No mean feat, when you're writing about yourself.

Olivia Laing, my new favorite nonfiction writer, has won a place in my heart as a direct result of those twin catastrophes, Trump and Brexit. (Really, spell-check? Brexit? Even after eighteen months and two billion uses of the word? I think you're going to have to sort yourself out, because it's not going away anytime soon.) I decided that if I wasn't going to spend all my time marching up and down and shouting at people (and I'm not, even though I accept that's probably the best response to it all), then I'm going to read, watch great movies and mediocre football, explore jazz, and live in my mind whenever I am able to. Laing is an embodiment of this anti-societal mood: she's surprising, nerdy, odd, passionate, a deep thinker, empathetic, raw, at home in just about every artistic discipline, a terrific critic, and an elegant writer. *The Lonely City* is about loneliness in art, a subject that she takes on because she herself is feeling lonely while she is exploring it, and a subject that throws up a wealth of extraordinarily rich material. There's Edward Hopper, whose cinemas and diners are filled with people on their own, and there's Warhol, an odd, lonely child whom Capote described as "the loneliest and most friendless person I'd ever met in my life." Most terrifying of all, there is Henry Darger, the extraordinary outsider artist whose desperate solitude was addressed with enigmatic indirectness in his wildly detailed collages and his fifteen-thousand-page novel, *In the Realms of the Unreal*. (He wrote two hundred and six pages of an autobiography before losing focus and turning it into a five-thousand-page story about a hurricane called Sweetie Pie.) The chapter on Darger is one of the best pieces of writing about art I've ever read: Laing's thoughts take her deep into the paintings but also into the works of Melanie Klein and the behavioral psychologist Harry Harlow, whose cruel experiments with monkeys revealed that a warm, soft touch is even more important to young animals than food. I haven't finished it yet, but I'm as happy as a clam reading about dysfunction and deep, unreachable sadness. I may dig a hole in the ground, pull a lid over it, and read the rest of *The Lonely City* in there. What's the alternative? ✳

APRIL/MAY 2018

BOOKS READ:

* ✶ *Vernon Subutex 1*—Virginie Despentes
* ✶ *"Astral Weeks": A Secret History of 1968*—Ryan H.Walsh
* ✶ *Voices: How a Great Singer Can Change Your Life*—Nick Coleman
* ✶ *The Line Becomes a River: Dispatches from the Border*—Francisco Cantú

BOOKS BOUGHT:

* ✶ *Fire and Fury: Inside the Trump White House*—Michael Wolff
* ✶ *To the River: A Journey Beneath the Surface*—Olivia Laing
* ✶ *Trouble Boys: The True Story of the Replacements*—Bob Mehr
* ✶ *Why I'm No Longer Talking to White People About Race*—Reni Eddo-Lodge
* ✶ *1947: When Now Begins*—Elisabeth Åsbrink
* ✶ *Three Daughters of Eve*—Elif Shafak
* ✶ *Grant & I: Inside and Outside the Go-Betweens*—Robert Forster
* ✶ *The Nix*—Nathan Hill

I turned sixty in 2017, and before I reached that dismal milestone, I was of the opinion that you're only as old as you feel, that age is just a number, that life is a box of chocolates, et cetera. I am working on the assumption that *Believer* readers had never even heard the number sixty before I mentioned it just now, and certainly had no idea that it could be an age human beings reach, so I bring you news from the far-distant future: there is indeed, as you might have suspected, a pill that men are forced to swallow on the last day they are fifty-nine that makes them less interested in new fiction. I tried to hide it in my cheek, but eventually—another peril of advancing years—I forgot it was sinister and swallowed it, thinking it was one of the other pills they give me here after dinner.

I try to find works of fiction, I promise, but it's like pushing a wonky shopping trolley round a supermarket. I constantly veer off toward literary biographies, books about the Replacements, and so on, and only with a concerted effort can I push it toward the best our novelists have to offer. I suspect it's to do with age and risk. A bad book about, say, the history of Indian railways will inevitably tell you something about railways, India, and history. Reading a bad novel when you are approaching pensionable age, however, is like taking the time left available to you and setting it on fire. (I am also getting the impression that most books by young novelists are about sexual abuse. I know, I know—I shouldn't be so squeamish. But I'm in the middle of an English winter, there's no daylight after about eleven o'clock in the morning, I've quite often watched my football team play out a dismal, goalless draw... Give me a break until the spring, at least.)

A couple of months ago I was at a literary festival in Germany, and tout le monde, and *alles der Welt*, was talking about *Vernon Subutex 1*, the first in an ambitious trilogy of novels by the French writer Virginie Despentes. I had never heard of it, or her, because I live in an English-speaking country that takes very little notice of fiction published in translation. Those of us in the US and the UK, even those who read, tend to regard foreign literature as entirely laudable—it's jolly good that these people have a go—but not for us. And yet here we all are, plodding dutifully through a six-hundred-page prizewinning novel written in our own language that we're not enjoying very much and that nobody will ever read again after the initial buzz has fizzled, while being utterly ignorant of what's happening in Germany or Italy (pace Ferrante) or France or entire continents.

Vernon Subutex is the hapless former owner of a Parisian record shop. The shop has gone bust, like most big-city music stores, and Vernon's luck and judgment have drained away to the point where he is homeless and penniless. His solution is ingenious: he calls all his former patrons, tells them he's been living in Canada and is back for a visit, and asks to stay on their sofas or in their spare bedrooms for a few nights. Despentes is thus free to write about contemporary Paris in all its social media–stained, spliff-addled, coke-pumped, money-obsessed, bitter, screenwriter-desperate, violent, racist shambles. Now, first of all, does that sound like a "novel in translation"? If we examine our prejudices—or, at least, if I examine mine on your behalf—they belong to a genre, something we can congratulate ourselves on reading. They frequently get their own spot in bookstores, unless they have somehow found some sort of readership, in which case we co-opt them as our own. You won't find Elena Ferrante or Stieg Larsson in this section. They have sold their way out of the ghetto.

Vernon Subutex 1 deserves a better fate too. It has a smart high concept—a little like *High Maintenance* in the way that doors are literally opened to the protagonist, although Ben Sinclair's "The Guy" is a lot sunnier, perhaps because pot is easier to sell than music, and he's not homeless, as far as we know. And it's peppered with references you will recognize, and some of them will make you chuckle with delight at their appearance in a literary novel: "Groove Is in the Heart," Cassandra Wilson, the Exploited, Thee Oh Sees, KitKat McFlurries... It's long, *Vernon Subutex 1*, and if I don't follow it through to the second and third in the sequence, then it's because I don't know how much appetite I have for the fury and the pitilessness of Despentes's singular worldview. But I'm very glad to have wrestled this one to the ground. I have never read Balzac, so the references for me were Dickens and the young Martin Amis: the teeming population, the grotesques, the relentlessness and energy of the narrative. I'm not sure Despentes has the same faith in social reform, however. Her Paris seems too far gone for that.

And then I'm sent a proof of Ryan H. Walsh's *"Astral Weeks": A Secret History of 1968* and suddenly I'm not wrestling at all. I'm drinking it down, too quickly, almost, and in part this is because Walsh has no need and can find no place for fury and pitilessness. Some of the characters you meet in this book are unsavory, granted, but the story he has unearthed is so mind-boggling, so full of extraordinary detail and coincidence and strange, now impossible ambitions, that one can only share in his delight at the sheer improbability of it all.

Where to begin? Van Morrison's celebrated album is part of it all, but it glides in and out of the book like a particularly lovely ghost. The record was shaped in Boston, and the songs were performed for the first time in a Boston club called the Catacombs in the summer of '68—Peter Wolf of the J. Geils Band, then a Boston R&B DJ who went by the name of the Woofa Goofa, has a tape of the show, although Nelson never gets to hear Wolf's copy. But mostly *"Astral Weeks"* is about why a grumpy cosmic Irishman like Morrison would end up in Cambridge in the first place, and it turns out that Boston was, for a while, completely and utterly loopy.

There was the experimental TV program *What's Happening, Mr. Silver?*, which on one memorable occasion asked viewers to place one TV set opposite another so the young British presenter, the eponymous David Silver, could interview a theater director in black and white on one screen, while on the other a color Silver provided a cynical running commentary on his own efforts. There was the Bosstown Sound, a desperate attempt to turn the city into a San Francisco or a Liverpool, and which resulted in too much money being paid to average, and green, musicians, and which also produced two touring versions of the Bosstown band Orpheus. (The phony version, which was playing without the knowledge or permission of the original band, featured a young Chevy Chase, but this is the sort of bizarre fact that becomes almost routine in Walsh's pages.) There was James Brown's concert the night after the assassination of Martin Luther King Jr., when the show was televised on a local station, and Brown was paid by the city for the shortfall in box-office sales, and everyone stayed home instead of going out and setting everything on fire.

If there is a central character in this book, it's not Morrison but Mel Lyman, a charismatic former folk-rock singer who led a commune, founded a terrifyingly alternative underground maga-zine, befriended—some might say brainwashed—the daughter of the epic painter Thomas Hart Benton, bought every house on a rundown Boston street, and invested in a Los Angeles construction company that still exists today. Lyman probably died, probably in the late '70s, although his death wasn't announced until 1985, and there is no death certificate; whether he was dead or alive, a lot of what was going on in Boston in the late 1960s was due to him. *Avatar*, the underground magazine, provoked an all-out war with the authorities, a war that Lyman had the money to fight—one of the witnesses for the defense, incidentally, was the young Howard Zinn.

Who else turns up? There's Michelangelo Antonioni, who cast one of Lyman's commune members as the lead in his first English-language movie, *Zabriskie Point*, after a casting director saw him get into an altercation at a bus stop. (Antonioni came to regret it.) There's Jonathan Richman, devoted fan of the Velvet Underground, who remade themselves after taking up semipermanent residency at the city's Fillmore-like venue the Boston Tea Party, and there's the Boston Strangler and Timothy Leary and Frederick Wiseman and and and... Possibly if you were to spend years investigating a crucial period in the life of your city, you would find stories as good and as rich as these, but even then you would have to have an eye as keen as Walsh's, a nose as sharp, an ear as sensitive and as attuned to the frequency of the times. This is a wonderful book, I think, funny and interesting and completely absorbing, if you have any interest in just about anything this magazine holds dear—art, politics, fun, music, chaos.

The excellence of the other two nonfiction books I read this month didn't help with the state of my current appetite for novels. Nick Coleman has written a brilliant book about singing, *Voices*, a simple title for a complicated subject. Can Bob Dylan sing? Of course he can, in the sense that he conveys feeling, thinks about his phrasing, knows how to turn some of the most memorable verses ever written into punches that sting. Can Frank Sinatra sing? Well, yes, that's not in doubt, although in his chapter on crooners, Coleman essays the puzzling question of why that particular voice leaves so many of us who came of listening age post-Beatles unmoved and uninvolved. These essays are about vulnerable voices (Amy Winehouse's, Aretha's, Mary Margaret O'Hara's), prayerful voices (Van's again, Burning Spear), English voices (Ray Davies's, Mick Jagger's, David Bowie's), the voices of people who sing through brass instruments (Hank Mobley). There's an idea on every single page, and sometimes you may want to argue with the mind behind it, but then, *Voices* wants your engagement. And such is the clarity of thought and efficacy of expression that you'll need to be right at the top of your game to make a point that hasn't been anticipated. I have been talking to Nick Coleman about music, in person and in my head, for forty years now, and though you can get only a tiny sliver of my good luck through both this book and his beautiful memoir, *The Train in the Night: A Story of Music and Loss*, you at least have the opportunity to hear what I have heard. I hope you take it.

The music in Francisco Cantú's *The Line Becomes a River* is in the prose, and gosh, it's sad. Cantú is a gifted, sensitive memoirist who worked for five years as a border patrol agent, and the painful collision of those two incompatible sensibilities has produced a brave, affecting, memorable book. Am I saying it's impossible to be both sensitive and a border patrol agent? No—Cantú is. His job involves stopping people from joining up with their families, and trying to save the lives of those who have set out across the desert without enough food or water—for themselves or, sometimes, for their children—and picking up dirt-poor juvenile Mexicans who are on their way to the US to sell heroin. People are sent over the border by narcos—because bodies are, like drugs, worth something to somebody—and then held captive in safe houses, fifteen or twenty to a room, until a loved one is prepared to pay something for their release. It's an unstoppable tide of human misery, and Cantú is plagued by dreams—dreams of wolves, of crumbling teeth. They feel real enough to the reader, let alone the dreamer. At the end of the book Cantú is working in a coffee shop while enrolled in an MFA program. When a colleague goes back over the border to see his dying mother, leaving his wife and two boys behind, and doesn't come back, Cantú does what he can to help his friend cut through the bureaucracy, but the branches are too thick; at this point, Cantú hands the narrative over to José, and the anguish of his situation is allowed to ring out clear and true, and so loud that even we can hear it. One good thing, amid all the unhappiness: in the author photo, Cantú is wearing a bolo tie, and he looks cool in it, and I bought one and wore it on New Year's Eve. Thank you, Francisco.

Oh, what to do about fiction, when nonfiction is so reliably good? Maybe I should go back to reading old novels. That might be the answer. Read a book by a young novelist and you end up saying to yourself, No, young fella or young lady. That's not what people are like. Read a book written in the '50s or the '20s or the nineteenth century and you think, Wow, that's what people were like? The particular psychology of a moment, the sort of thing fiction is so good at capturing, is preserved only within the pages of novels, which gives the oldies a distinct advantage: you can't argue with them. Of course, back in the nineteenth century, old codgers like me were probably reading George Eliot and grumbling about her inability to portray real nineteenth-century people. But we'll never know. STOP PRESS: I started a novel on the Tube this morning. The first ten pages were great. I'll let you know. ✶

JUNE/JULY 2018

BOOKS READ:

★ *Trouble Boys: The True Story of the Replacements*—Bob Mehr
★ *To Throw Away Unopened*—Viv Albertine
★ *Who Is Rich?*—Matthew Klam
★ *The Adulterants*—Joe Dunthorne

BOOKS BOUGHT:

★ *The Littlehampton Libels: A Miscarriage of Justice and a Mystery About Words in 1920s England*— Christopher Hilliard
★ *Janesville: An American Story*—Amy Goldstein
★ *Why We Sleep: Unlocking the Power of Sleep and Dreams*—Matthew Walker

Fathers: can't live with them, can't exist without them. The father of Bob Stinson, guitarist of the Replacements, was a boozer who lost touch with his kids when he split up with their mother. Bob's younger half brother, Tommy's father, was also a boozer who sexually, physically, and verbally abused his stepchildren. Bob's second stepfather was merely a mean drunk. Bob was in and out of care homes and dead at thirty-five. Viv Albertine's father was a jealous, violent bully who made his wife give up her child from a previous marriage. The Stinsons and Albertine both went on to make glorious, significant, provocative rock music.

The title of Bob Mehr's sympathetic, gripping, exhaustive, and occasionally exhausting book about the history of the Replacements, *Trouble Boys*, is missing a *d* from the end of the first word of its title: these boys were troubled long before they formed a band, and carried on being troubled long after it had split up. Drugs and especially drink were both the symptom and the cause of it all, but this was not the glamorous, Keith Richards version of dependency, the sort that makes rock critics swoon, nor was it the Faces' laddish determination to bring their local pub onstage with them every night. This was the nasty, mean, inexplicably self-destructive version, with blackouts and puking and broken marriages.

If you're unfamiliar with the work of the Replacements, it's probably too late now, but they meant a lot to me and people like me in the 1980s, when punk rock was dead and guitars were hard to hear among all the Syndrums and keyboards. Songwriter Paul Westerberg's best songs have an ache to them that couldn't be smothered by volume or self-destruction. The band competed with REM and lost, and were then swept away by Nirvana's tide. I loved them, but I didn't think I wanted to read four hundred pages about them; however, Mehr's book is so clear-eyed, and the stories are so extraordinary, that it was gone in a flash.

Tommy Stinson was thirteen when the Replacements formed. His brother had bullied and cajoled him into picking up the bass a couple of years before, partly because Bob needed a bassist, and partly because Tommy was already well down the road to delinquency that Bob had already walked. When the band started to tour and record, Tommy left school and never went back. Thirteen! I am still not old enough to live the life that Tommy Stinson embarked upon, but my thirteen-year-old self would have been dead within the first twelve hours—killed by fear and shock, probably, rather than vodka, which would have gotten me a couple of hours later. Tommy was drinking heavily by his mid-teens, and groupies regarded him as an underage prize. By the time he joined Guns N' Roses in 1998, at age thirty-two, long after the Replacements were no more, he had been living a Guns N' Roses lifestyle for nearly two decades.

This isn't a story about how the music industry destroyed a band. The music industry loved them, mostly, and they had friends and supporters in high places. The Replacements took every opportunity that was offered to them, spit on it, and chucked it straight through the window.

Record company execs who turned up at a prestigious CBGB gig were treated to drunken covers of "Jolene," "You're a Mean One, Mr. Grinch," an obscene version of "The Ballad of Jed Clampett," a whistled version of the theme song to *The Andy Griffith Show*, and one of Elvis Presley's less celebrated songs, "Do the Clam," sung by a roadie. The audience was mostly gone before the end of the set.

They were banned forever from *Saturday Night Live* for shouting an obscenity during their performance. Always broke, Westerberg and Tommy Stinson repeatedly set fire to their per diems—in the literal sense of the phrase, with matches. Invited to open for Tom Petty, they insulted the audience, played interminable covers of "Walk on the Wild Side," and insulted the headliner in front of his fans. It is fair to say they weren't cute drunks.

When a fan made Tommy Stinson a bass guitar and presented it to him before the show, Tommy played the first song of the set with it, and then smashed it to pieces before the guy's eyes, sending a message to everyone who had any time for them: *You may think you love us, but you can't. You may think you're on our side, but you're not. We're the only people who are on our side.* Perhaps that explains the ache in Westerberg's songs: there was a loneliness that could never be reached, and a blazing talent that could never be truly fulfilled. But Paul Westerberg and Tommy Stinson are still around, still making music, still heard; that didn't seem to be the way their lives were going back when they were young.

The bad behavior described in Viv Albertine's *To Throw Away Unopened* cannot be blamed only on drink and drugs. But the crimes of useless fathers, it seems, have to be paid for by the next generation, in some currency or other. Some of the memoir takes place on the night Albertine's mother died, which happened to be the night that her previous book—also a memoir, also worth your time and attention, and also written about in these pages—was launched. The astonishing events of that evening form the spine of the book; the flesh is provided by an account of her parents' marriage, and by wry, occasionally baffling tales of Albertine's attempts to fill a gap in her own life with a partner of some description.

Certainly, it is difficult to describe Eryk, who goes to bed with Albertine fully clothed, socks and all, and will let her undo only the top button of his shirt. The relationship proceeds slowly and, it has to be said, somewhat eccentrically: "Eryk and I went on quite a few dates, but as he avoided intimate encounters I still hadn't undone all the buttons on his shirt or seen his penis after knowing him for six months." One promising night, after long, long kisses, he grabs a copy of Wilkie Collins's *The Woman in White* and starts reading it out loud. If I had known the author, I feel I might have been able to tell her that Eryk might well turn out to be a dud, sexually speaking, and that she should at least lower her expectations. But he pops up again toward the end of the book, with Albertine hopeful about a romantic weekend in a seaside hotel. It turns out to be a disappointment. Sex, said Johnny Rotten, is "two minutes and fifty-two seconds of squelching"; Albertine, a contemporary of Rotten's when she was in the Slits, seems to feel much the same way.

Such is the richness of the material Albertine has at her disposal that *To Throw Away Unopened* is not even about Eryk, even though I would have been happy to read several hundred more pages about him. It is about the brutal nature of her parents' marriage, in the light of not one but two diaries, his and hers, that Albertine finds after their deaths. These diaries were kept during the last two years of their disintegrating marriage, at the suggestion of their lawyers. There was no such thing as a "no-fault" divorce during the 1960s. Our sympathies sway from mother to father and back again, but in the end it's Albertine's indomitable, unhappy mother, Kathleen, whose truth rings the loudest.

And yet—stop me if you've heard this before—such is the richness of the material Albertine has at her disposal that *To Throw Away Unopened* is not even about et cetera, et cetera. Or rather, it's not the story that you will think of first when you press this book into a friend's hands, as you undoubtedly will. On the night of her mother's death—*in the hospital room in which her mother is dying*—Viv and her sister Pascale have an altercation so violent that blood is spilled, by both warring parties, and spilled onto the woman to whom they have come to say goodbye. It's so serious that a couple of weeks later the police call, asking Viv if she wants to press charges. You can tell that a deathbed scene is not going according to plan when the most useful piece of advice you can remember is "To get a pit bull to unclamp its jaws, insert two fingers into its nostrils and pull upwards."

I don't think I have ever read a memoir like this. Albertine's tone is cool, occasionally quizzical, without either self-pity or blame, so to read it is to enter a parallel universe where its narrative incidents are somehow rendered comprehensible and almost routine. It also manages to be about things we might connect to—men and women, marriages, parenthood, the follies and tragedies of the generation before mine—when it could be excused for being only about things we can scarcely believe. I think you may have to read it.

Last month, I was despairing about my relationship with fiction, and even though *Trouble Boys* and *To Throw Away Unopened* contain such gripping real-life tales that they might have dulled my appetite for novels even further, I read two excellent ones, Joe Dunthorne's *The Adulterants* and Matthew Klam's *Who Is Rich?* Both are about errant husbands, although Dunthorne's is too hapless to err very far; both are funny; both are fresh; both seem effortlessly pertinent. They have different strengths and no discernible weaknesses. And, strikingly, given the inadequacy of the dads in the two nonfiction books, the commitment of these otherwise hapless men to their children is not in doubt. Maybe that's what we have learned from our predecessors: when it comes to parenting, absence does not make the heart grow fonder. I grew up with an absent father, and as a consequence my own children will be able only to complain about my presence. I am sure they will do this long and loudly—*He was always there! He never left the house!*—and probably to therapists, but at least I will have bucked the trend.

Klam's book is set over a long weekend at an arts conference. Rich Fischer, the eponymous and impoverished antihero, is a cartoonist who had a hit with his first autobiographical graphic novel and now has nothing much to say, but is desperate to say it. In the meantime, he illustrates for a prestigious magazine and watches while other, younger rivals are showered with devotion and advances. He had taught at this particular New England retreat the previous summer, and met a woman named Amy. Amy is not his wife; his wife is at home, earning the money that he isn't, and looking after their young children. She is tired, and he is tired; his sad annual affair with Amy, who is married to a boorish and unloving multimillionaire, is the product of everybody's exhaustion. Before you hate Rich too much, he doesn't get an enormous amount of pleasure from cheating on his wife. In the words of Commander Cody's great song "Too Much Fun": "There must be a whole lotta things that I never done, / but I ain't never had too much fun."

The genius of Klam's book is in its details. The author has imagined every millimeter of Rich's terrain, emotional and physical—his bitter, anxious colleagues at the conference, the hospital room where Amy and Rich have sex after Amy has broken her arm, both of them bombed out of their heads on painkillers, the seaside town where the conference takes place: "Two men ate ice-cream in booty shorts under a sign advertising a drag show, beside a store selling taffy, a store selling kitchen gadgets. A guy in tight teal jeans drank coffee with a woman with jingly gypsy sandals outside a bar smelling of fried oysters. An elderly woman with gray dreadlocks buzzed by in an electric wheelchair led by dogs in rainbow collars. In this town even dogs could be gay." Klam didn't need to write any of that, but he can see it, and we see better for it. There's something about the dark energy powering this book which reminds me of David Gates, whose two novels *Jernigan* and *Preston Falls* are forgotten classics of the very late twentieth century. In fact, I know we're only at the beginning of a *siècle*, but *Who Is Rich?* feels very fin de siècle, as the entire bohemian middle-class world, which used to be able to make some kind of living and look the outside world in the eye, falls to pieces.

Joe Dunthorne's third novel is, I think, better than his first two, and his first two—*Submarine* (adapted for a very charming indie movie) and *Wild Abandon*—were really good. He's the sort of writer I'm always looking for and can rarely find: his work is funny, truthful, has depth and soul, and he can't write a long book to save his life. He's a fine poet, too, but those skills are used for the precision and pin-sharp, dry tone here, and some very funny aphorisms, rather than pages of waffle about trees, which is what one always fears about poets' novels.

The Adulterants begins with the narrative incident that sends tech journalist Ray's life spiraling out of control: he gets punched, hard, by a friend, after an incident with said friend's partner. His wife, Garthene, is pregnant, and he loves her: "Garthene's head, at a guess, had the dimensions of a child's shoebox. I adored this about her and looked forward to our retirement when her hair's thinning would reveal further nuances. The fact that I would never guess the exact shape was one of the ways in which our marriage would stay fresh." This, surely, is a definition of love, and yet without spoiling things too much, it still isn't enough. Single heterosexual women: if you think that finding a man who looks forward to seeing the shape of your head when you have no hair is the answer, think again.

The long and the short of it is that, because of Matthew Klam and Joe Dunthorne, I love fiction again, and will read some more. (And next month I won't be writing about authors with names like Joe and Matthew, either. This column will be full of Jennifers and Elizabeths and, and... Georges, if I read any George Eliot, which is looking unlikely.) But I also love nonfiction, and will read some more. Conclusion: all kinds of good books are good. It took me a couple of thousand words to get there, but I hope I've left you something to think about. ✷

AUGUST/SEPTEMBER 2018

BOOKS READ:
- ✶ *The Female Persuasion*—Meg Wolitzer
- ✶ *Conversations with Friends*—Sally Rooney
- ✶ *Crudo*—Olivia Laing
- ✶ *Little Fires Everywhere*—Celeste Ng
- ✶ *How to Listen to Jazz*—Ted Gioia

BOOKS BOUGHT:
- ✶ *The New Testament*—Jericho Brown
- ✶ *There Are More Beautiful Things Than Beyoncé*—Morgan Parker
- ✶ *Something Wonderful: Rodgers and Hammerstein's Broadway Revolution*—Todd S. Purdum

"The culture has changed over the years," explained former British defense secretary Michael Fallon, following his resignation from the Cabinet after repeatedly placing his hand on the knee of a female journalist. "What might have been acceptable ten years ago is clearly not acceptable now." Fallon resigned in November 2017, so he is talking about those heady years between 2002 and 2007, years mostly lost to the mists of time, when Taylor Swift's songs were country inflected, we watched all five seasons of *The Wire*, and it was perfectly acceptable for a gentleman to grope a lady without asking for permission first. "I came of age in the '60s and '70s, when all the rules about behavior and workplaces were different," said Harvey Weinstein, whose job description and crimes need no explanation here. "That was the culture then."

Perhaps the eagle-eyed reader will see a theme developing: before all you women came along with your aggressive hashtags, anything went, and nobody minded. Indeed, not only did nobody mind, but everyone—men and women—was probably happier.

What enrages me about this particular line of defense is that I was born five years after Fallon and Weinstein, who were both born in 1952, and in my entire lifetime it has never been OK to behave in the way that these men have. I went to college in the 1970s, and several workplaces in the 1980s, and I knew how to behave, not because of any inmate moral sense or enlightened parenting, but because the writers and thinkers of generations before mine had done the work for me. Germaine Greer had written *The Female Eunuch*; Gloria Steinem was famous; *Spare Rib*, the influential British feminist magazine, was available in any bookshop; Virago publishing had been founded; there were Reclaim the Night marches. The Au Pairs released the single "It's Obvious"—"You're equal, but different, you're equal, but different, it's obvious"—in 1980, and everyone I knew could sing it. Michael Fallon was an English public (private) schoolboy who probably didn't meet a woman until he had his own secretary, but Harvey Weinstein knew about all of this stuff. Feminism wasn't some kind of arcane belief with three disciples at UC Berkeley; it was mainstream, and every man was aware of it. If you chose to remain a pig, it was because it was easier and more gratifying that way, not because you didn't know any better.

Meg Wolitzer's novel *The Female Persuasion* is about the #MeToo generation, but it's also about the women who schooled me. I have no idea whether Wolitzer's young heroine, Greer, is any kind of a nod to the author of *The Female Eunuch*, but in any case the older generation is represented by Faith Frank, a Germaine-like figure whose writing and insight have influenced and inspired generations of women, and Greer turns out to be no exception: when she meets Faith after a lecture at her college, her life is changed profoundly.

The spine of the narrative is an account of the relationship between Faith and Greer over a decade. It's about the older woman's spell over her admirer; and disillusionment; and compromise; and where feminism is at, where it's been, where it's going. The novel could not be any more timely, even though its length and the completeness of its world suggest to me that it must have been conceived before the recent upheavals and protests.

So you'll want to read it for all the above reasons, I should think, but all the above does not begin to convey the sweep or emotional power of *The Female Persuasion*. I cannot tell you how much I loved and continue to love this book. Actually, I'm going to have a go because, after all, that's what I'm supposed to do, and if I couldn't I wouldn't be much use to you.

I am a huge admirer of Meg Wolitzer's work—*The Wife* is one of my favorite novels of the twenty-first century—but *The Female Persuasion* has gone straight into my library of favorite novels ever, on a shelf next to *David Copperfield, Dinner at the Homesick Restaurant, Lonesome Dove,* and *Love in the Time of Cholera.* (These shelves are not alphabetized. Rather, the books are just allowed to sit there, secure in the knowledge that they are loved and will always be loved. Nor are they limited by number. There will always be room for another one.) Right from the opening pages of *The Female Persuasion*, I could feel its world close me in, like a stadium with a retractable roof that keeps the rain off when there's a storm; to focus merely on the theme of the book—if feminism can be said to be the theme rather than a theme—is to exclude the stuff that makes it so memorable. Wolitzer has also written a compelling and touching love story, between Greer and her childhood friend Corey, and a wonderful examination of female friendship, between Greer and her gay college friend Zee. Wolitzer's characters are imagined from every angle, and loved by their creator, in the way that God is supposed to love us: with a steady, knowing, occasionally pained gaze.

When Greer begins to work for Faith Frank, Zee writes Faith a letter asking for a job and gives it to Greer to pass on. Greer can't bring herself to do it, for reasons that are entirely human and, I'm ashamed to say, completely recognizable: she doesn't want to share the relationship she has with her mentor. When Corey endures a shattering domestic tragedy, he locks himself for a very long time out of the world he had started to create for himself. Misery is hardly a fresh subject in literary fiction, but I can't recall it ever being handled with the perspicacity that Wolitzer demonstrates here; it's usually enough for novelists to demonstrate its existence. Very few have ideas and observations about it. And this, now that I come to think about it, is what Wolitzer does throughout this book. She wants to know what all of these things—ambition, feminism, friendship, love, idealism, cynicism, compromise—say about us. So, yes, *The Female Persuasion* is about the way we live now, but it's also about how we have always lived. That's a great novel, by my definition.

I loved *The Female Persuasion* with such passion that I don't think I'll recommend it to everybody. I'd be too afraid that the wrong sort of person would respond in a way that demonstrated their inadequacies, as a reader and as a human being. So be warned: if we meet one day, and we talk about books, and I don't mention this one, it's because I think you might be an arse.

I read *Conversations with Friends* immediately after *The Female Persuasion*, and for a while I struggled with the gear change. Rooney was born in 1991, while I was writing my first book, but to my enormous credit I don't hate her. It's pretty hard to hate her, unfortunately, because she's clearly brilliant, and just about every page of *Conversations with Friends* demonstrates that she's in it for the long haul. She won't always be a hot new talent, of course, but that isn't going to matter to her, because that hot new talent is built on a very sturdy foundation.

One of the reviews quoted on the paperback describes *Conversations with Friends* as "a hugely enjoyable romantic comedy," and if this was the only review Rooney had received (and it wasn't—there are hundreds of them), she might not have found her readership. This isn't *Bridget Jones's Diary*. Frances, the book's narrator, cuts herself, sleeps with a married man whose wife she knows well, suffers from a painful and incurable disease, exposes and hurts her closest friend and former partner through her writing. She's terse and acerbic, and she spends a lot of the book pinching herself so she can feel something.

This was the gear change—Wolitzer's characters display kindness and a firm moral direction at almost every step; after all, moral purpose is embedded in the narrative. Rooney's characters are aware of the theory—they are students, writers, artists, and they talk about cultural theories of monogamy and Gilles Deleuze (a name, I regret to confess, that was unfamiliar to me; so not only was Sally Rooney born in 1991, but she knows more than I do).

None of this, however, describes the spirit of the book. Rooney isn't lost inside this stuff; she floats above it, with a writer's grace and observational power, and even though the generation she writes about is profoundly different from my own, *Conversations with Friends* felt both true and wise. And, writer friends: it contains this very lovely description of the joy of revising one's work: "I could see the story I had written gaining shape, unfolding itself, becoming longer and more solid." That little phrase "unfolding itself" is so perfect: anyone who's tried to write anything will know exactly that feeling, when ideas and narrative fragments are trapped in the fabric, and a little more room allows them to breathe. Frances, we can see, will be a writer one day; Sally Rooney could not have written those words if she wasn't already a writer, an extremely good one. I can't wait for her next novel.

I believe I told you in the last issue of this magazine that I was going to read novels by women, and so scrupulously have I kept my promise that I might have gone too far the other way. (Note to anyone likely to take offense: I was kidding. There's no such thing as "too far the other way." Even if I read only books by women for the rest of my life, I could not atone for the sins of my gender.) (Note to anyone: possibly the same people who were about to point out that there's no such thing as "too far the other way," who regard the previous note as some kind of confession: I plead not guilty to all the sins of my gender. Some, but not all, and the ones I plead guilty to I regard as minor misdemeanors. But of course I would think that.) *Anyway*, I have read only fiction by women this month, and because I want to write about Ted Gioia, I have very little space to praise Olivia Laing and Celeste Ng.

Crudo is the third book I've read by Olivia Laing in the last twelve months, so she can't complain about the space she's been given in these pages. I praised her brilliant books of memoir-cum-criticism, *The Trip to Echo Spring* and *The Lonely City*, to the heavens, but I didn't overdo it, because they're both brilliant. *Crudo* is her first novel, and it begins: "Kathy, by which I mean I, was getting married. Kathy, by which I mean I, had just got off a plane from New York." (You won't see this, of course, but the first *which* is being queried by my in-computer grammarian, who has given it a wavy green line, while it hasn't done the same for the second *which*. I have no idea why.)

"Kathy" is Kathy Acker, the experimental post-punk novelist; "I" is Olivia Laing. The two are somehow welded together in ways I enjoyed but didn't entirely understand. Laing's experiment, and it's a good one, is to describe the world—her world, between May 17 and September 23, 2017—as precisely as she can. FBI directors get fired, dictators with nuclear weapons make threats, London tower blocks burn, I/Kathy gets married on the day Steve Bannon resigns, as Olivia Laing did. It's a short, entirely readable, and lovably eccentric book that may well— one day, when we, or more likely they, all want to know about that mad year as it was *felt*—serve its purpose precisely. Celeste Ng's *Little Fires Everywhere* I'm guessing you might have read already, in which case you already know that it's beautifully written, completely charming, and extremely wise on the subject of adolescence and influence.

It is, perhaps, unfortunate that the one book I've read by a man is entitled *How to Listen to Jazz*. A guy giving instructions on how to do something that you either didn't want to do or could do anyway… Need I even type out the neologism invented to describe exactly this behavior? If you do have an interest in jazz, however, please try to think of it as a book entitled *Stuff You Didn't Know About Jazz but Would Like To*. I know quite a lot about jazz now, after an epiphany I described in these pages a few years ago, and I found it both inspiring and informative. Listening to Fats Waller's "Sidewalk Blues" while reading Gioa's breakdown of its structure, I got the kind of tingle that some nerds talk about getting when they reminisce about the teachers who changed their lives. I never had that sensation at school or at college, but it's happening more and more in later life as I learn about the things that mean the most to me. It could, of course, be that I'm having lots of little strokes, but either way it feels good. ✳

OCTOBER/NOVEMBER 2018

BOOKS READ:

* ★ *Something Wonderful: Rodgers and Hammerstein's Broadway Revolution*—Todd S. Purdum
* ★ *The Order of Time*—Carlo Rovelli
* ★ *The Incurable Romantic and Other Unsettling Revelations*—Frank Tallis
* ★ *The Queen's Gambit*—Walter Tevis

BOOKS BOUGHT:

* ★ *The Secret Life of the American Musical: How Broadway Shows Are Built*—Jack Viertel
* ★ *The Incurable Romantic and Other Unsettling Revelations*—Frank Tallis
* ★ *Making Oscar Wilde*—Michèle Mendelssohn
* ★ *The Friend*—Sigrid Nunez
* ★ *Love Sick: Love as a Mental Illness*—Frank Tallis
* ★ *Otis Redding: An Unfinished Life*—Jonathan Gould
* ★ *Prairie Fires: The American Dreams of Laura Ingalls Wilder*—Caroline Fraser

Where to start? One book I read this month challenges everything I, and perhaps even you, assumed about time and space; another is a joint biography of the men who wrote *Oklahoma!*, *Carousel*, and *South Pacific*. Which of these two is more important to us here at *The Believer*? Well, there's no real argument, is there? This magazine, or this column, anyway, believes that while second-act problems in musical theater productions are perhaps not everything, they are certainly more important than mind-boggling ideas about the way we understand the stupid universe.

Something Wonderful is above all a marvelous book about the arts and the artistic process. Todd S. Purdum provides a more than satisfying biography of Rodgers and Hammerstein, their successes and failures, their marriages, their money. But he's just as comfortable, and very acute, writing about their craft. He points out, for example, that "Oh What a Beautiful Mornin," the opening number of *Oklahoma!*, the first show they wrote together, takes the shape of a folk ballad, rather than a thirty-two-bar musical number, and that the repeated lines ("There's a bright golden haze on the meadow. / There's a bright golden haze on the meadow") are borrowed from the stylistically appropriate field holler tradition. The whole of *Oklahoma!* was a stylistic risk. The story, songs, and choreography were all entwined in a way that Broadway hadn't seen before, effectively creating the model we have been watching ever since. And like *Hamilton*, you would have had more luck getting a job in the chorus than a ticket to see it.

Comparisons to *Hamilton* are not spurious. Every time a new Rodgers and Hammerstein show is launched, you think, Huh. That's a crazy subject for a piece of musical entertainment—whether it's the formation of a new state, or the relationship between a governess and a king, or the grim poverty of the life of a fairground barker, or the interactions of American servicemen and South Sea islanders. And then you remember *Evita*, and *Les misérables*, and *Assassins*, and you realize that almost the first law of musicals is that the subject matter must always be unlikely. Not only did Rodgers and Hammerstein write musicals that worked; they stuffed them full of songs that will probably survive as long as popular music survives. "Oh What a Beautiful Mornin," "You'll Never Walk Alone," "Happy Talk," "I'm Gonna Wash That Man Right Out of My Hair," "I Cain't Say No," "Hello Young Lovers," "My Favorite Things," "The Surrey with the Fringe on Top," "You Took Advantage of Me"… If you don't like the original-cast versions, maybe you'll appreciate the versions by John Coltrane, or Miles Davis, or Hank Mobley, or Lee Morgan. All those guys knew a good tune when they heard one.

On top of everything else, *Something Wonderful* has soul. The relationship between Rodgers and Hammerstein is effectively an entirely successful and redemptive second marriage for both of them. Rodgers was on the rebound from a stormy period with Lorenz Hart, who was in the process of drinking himself to death; Hammerstein had been working with Jerome Kern and others, and had endured a decade of dismal failure before *Oklahoma!* He was all washed-up at forty-six, before the twenty spectacularly successful years that were to come. If you need people to root for in a book, then these two provide this in spades. I'm happy to have read this book, and I was also extremely happy while I was reading it. It's a very happy book, and you can't say that about everything you read.

I would like to tell you I that I listen to the BBC weekly radio show *The Life Scientific* with enormous attention, because I am a curious-minded individual as at ease in the worlds of immunology and genetics as in musical theater. But I actually listen to, or rather hear, the program because it's on shortly after 9 a.m., I haven't yet turned the radio off after the news, and I'm still wandering round and round the kitchen looking for keys, spectacles, and bottles of Heavenly Vanilla Custard vape juice before leaving for my office. But a few weeks ago the Italian quantum physicist Carlo Rovelli said the following:

> It is known for a fact that Newtonian time is wrong. The idea that time forms a long line, there's a now, a yesterday, a last year, a next year…
> We know for sure this is a bad picture. There's no line.

Well, that was news to me, pretty much. ("Pretty much"! Who am I kidding? I just put "pretty much" in there to suggest I had nibbled away at the edge of this knowledge-cake, picked the icing off, as it were. But I have left it untouched. I may as well be a diabetic when it comes to science-cakes.) That was news to me. Rovelli works at the Planck scale, where things are a billion trillion times smaller than the smallest atomic nucleus, which is in itself a million millionth of a millimeter. "Is it smaller than a sand? Is it smaller than a salt?" Ali G once said incredulously to a nuclear scientist. *Smaller than a salt?* By my estimate, a billion trillion million millionth of a millimeter is much smaller than a salt.

I was sufficiently dumbfounded by everything Rovelli was saying to go out and buy his book *The Order of Time*. But here's the truly impressive thing: once I bought it, I read it, apart from the two chapters he said I could skip if I found them heavy going. (I admit I didn't try that hard to come to grips with them. At that point, Rovelli had become the kind of teacher who says to his students, *Well, if you really don't think you can manage the homework tonight, don't do it.*)

Rovelli is a wonderful writer, and so even when you (or perhaps I should just stick to the first-person singular) don't know what's going on, he comes up with enjoyable, occasionally beautiful metaphors to help you (me). Time is not like "the English at a bus-stop, forming an orderly queue"; rather, it's a "crowd of Italians." And "the difference between things and events is that *things* persist in time; *events* have a limited duration. A stone is a prototypical 'thing': we can ask where it will be tomorrow. Conversely, a kiss is an 'event.' It makes no sense to ask where the kiss will be tomorrow." All rather lovely, but then you have to come to terms with Rovelli's assertion that, actually, they are no things: "The world is made up of networks of kisses, not of stones." Even a stone, it turns out, is an event, since it won't be around forever.

In the first few chapters, Rovelli does a good job of demolishing time: there's no present; there's no unity, because time is literally different at different altitudes or speeds, and it doesn't flow independently of us. These are all facts, I'm afraid. The stories we tell ourselves about time passing, about now and then and tomorrow, are not accurate; they are merely convenient, because we're still working on the story that will make sense to science. Newtonian time still works for us because we don't know any better, in the same way that a flat earth made sense to our primitive ancestors.

The ideas in *The Order of Time* are extraordinary, and I rather fear you should read it. It has, however, made me a more committed Newtonian. Let's face it: Newtonian time is going to do me for the rest of my natural life; I will continue to think of English queues rather than Italians jostling, because it makes life easier. By the time you are old, young *Believer* reader, you will probably be at ease with events and kisses, but I'm too set in my ways, and I can't deal in Planck time, because I've only just learned how to use Spotify properly. Good luck to you, but I can't say I envy you. The trouble with quantum physics is that it's a thrilling mind-fuck, and clearly dizzyingly important, but if you choose to ignore it, nothing will happen to you. You'll still be talking about last night's takeout, and the 2006 Champions League Final, and tomorrow's workday.

Psychotherapist Frank Tallis's *The Incurable Romantic and Other Unsettling Revelations* is also about a world we know but that is still completely alien to us—if we're lucky. We are familiar with heartbreak, separation, romantic yearning and dissatisfaction, sexual desire. But Tallis's book is about what happens when these perfectly ordinary feelings become warped, excessive, and unmanageable in some of his patients, and as you can imagine, it's pretty gripping. Megan, for example, was a barrister's clerk who needed a tooth extracted. When she came round after general anesthesia, she was in love with Damon, the doctor who had performed the surgery. She was also convinced that Damon was in love with her, and that all protestations to the contrary were merely indicative of his passion. She wrote him letters; she waited outside his surgery. Her husband was upset; Damon's wife became angry and threatened to call the police; she was put on medication that seemed only to intensify her feelings. In the end, he moved to Dubai. Megan had to settle for a little shrine—a newspaper cutting from a local paper, a paper clip, other things that Damon might have touched. All this time she remained married. Megan was and perhaps still is suffering from what was once known as De Clerambault syndrome, although nowadays it is more commonly referred to as erotomania. G. G. De Clerambault's most famous patient was a woman who was convinced that King George V was in love with her, and that he communicated with her by moving the curtains. It is extraordinary, the stories people will tell themselves. (By the way, the singer Shakira communicates with me by blinking as she sings certain key words during performances, but that is a practical necessity rather than a fantasy. We're both busy people.)

Meanwhile, Ali, a successful businessman with a wife and four children, came to see Tallis because his wife found evidence that he had been seeing a prostitute. Ali and Tallis danced around each other for a few weeks, until eventually Ali confessed that this wasn't the first time, or the first hooker. "It's actually closer to three thousand," he said. "Maybe more." He was not only sleeping with these women but convincing them that they had a future with him. "We'd chat about what our lives were going to be like, together. We'd go to see big houses, with an estate agent—and get really excited." Well, nobody can accuse him of being a commitment-phobe. The great thing about *The Incurable Romantic* is that it makes you feel better about yourself. Whether you're happily or unhappily married, happily or unhappily single, involved in an adulterous relationship with another person or even several other people, you're doing better than these guys.

The love lives of others are endlessly fascinating, but one of the points Tallis makes is that when we fall in love, we flirt with madness anyway. We are nuts about someone, or insanely jealous. We render ourselves temporarily incompetent, and find ourselves doing things that make sense only within the context of our passionate disturbance. And just as there are some unfortunate people who never come back after an acid trip and end up living in a tree for a decade or so, every time we become consumed by another, we run the risk of failing to make it to the far shore of contented domesticity, and of getting stranded in turbulent waters.

I read only one novel this month, Walter Tevis's ruinously gripping *The Queen's Gambit*. I was reminded of it by Michael Chabon's recent praise of the novel in an English newspaper. I had first read it when it came out, in 1983. Tevis is also the author of *The Hustler* and *The Man Who Fell to Earth*, both triumphantly filmed, and that is how I discovered him, in my early twenties. *The Queen's Gambit* is probably unfilmable because it is about chess, and there are blow-by-blow descriptive passages that are long enough for a *Kirkus* reviewer to describe it, upon its release, as an "on-and-off beguilement."[1] Well, it's not. It's just on, every page of it. I don't and can't play chess, but Tevis's obvious love for and understanding of the game allow him to distinguish every match that his heroine, Beth Harmon, plays from its predecessor. Some games are as clear as the clearest Mediterranean Sea; some are as murky as the English Channel. Some require more concentration than any of us have at our disposal; some just seem like feats of brute mental strength.

Beth Harmon is a chess prodigy who discovers her gift in the most unpromising circumstances: she plays in the basement with the caretaker of the orphanage where she lives. Tevis accomplishes many extraordinary things in this spare book, not the least of which is to make a novel set during the 1950s and '60s and written in the '80s feel as though it were a product of the #MeToo movement. The author never forgets that he's writing about a young woman in a dark-suited men's world, and his sympathy is almost bewilderingly contemporary.

What a few weeks I've had with my books. Actually, I don't suppose I'm allowed to say "a few weeks." Carlo Rovelli would tell me I've had a few kisses, and that those kisses are now jumbling around me like midges. Well, either way, they're still there in my mind—the books and the weeks. I'm not sure whether Planck time or Newtonian time applies to readers. We're lucky that way. ✶

---

1. Editor's Note: Hornby's prophecy here was, uncharacteristically, incorrect. As many know, *The Queen's Gambit* became a hugely popular Netflix series in 2020.

DECEMBER 2018/JANUARY 2019

How and why did I spend a few weeks, mostly on vacation, immersed in the life and works of Rosamond Lehmann, an author I had never read before? I hadn't planned to read her, particularly. It just happened. I have been feeling sufficiently baffled by my dedication that I decided to retrace my steps, and I now see that the journey started a couple of years ago, on holiday in Dorset. My family and several others stay in a big house there every year, and one of the many reasons we keep going back is the little market town of Bridport. And while it is not strictly necessary to provide an account of Bridport's appeal before coming to grips with a Bloomsbury novelist who, as far as I know, never went anywhere near the place (Bridport, not Bloomsbury), I'm going to do it anyway.

Bridport contains two proper secondhand-book shops, an excellent independent bookshop, a decent Waterstones, a secondhand-record shop, and a fantastic hat shop called Snook's. I live in Islington, North London, and we've got a Waterstones and a secondhand-record shop. In other words, Bridport is now more interesting than North London, if we're talking about the Saturday retail experience. When I was young, I used to travel twenty-five miles to London so I could buy the books, records, and clothes I wanted; now it's the other way around. Nobody can afford to own an independent store in my city, and maybe not in yours, either, and as a consequence, surprises and hats have been rendered nearly impossible to find. This year I found in Bridport vinyl copies of albums I'd wanted by Buddy Rich, Bob Brookmeyer, Bob Florence, and Stan Kenton, among others, at a record fair in the back of a church, and a paperback copy of an old Charles Webb book I'd never come across; the summer before last, I bought a beautiful 1953 edition of Rosamond Lehmann's *The Echoing Grove* in one of the used-book stores. That was step one of three.

Step two: *The Echoing Grove* sat on a shelf, lovely but unopened, until this year, when I was looking at my shelves for holiday reading and picked up not *The Echoing Grove* but another unread book, a paperback copy of Selina Hastings's biography of Lehmann, obtained from I don't know where, very possibly Bridport. It looked great, garlanded with quotes about its readability and gossip and charm and wisdom, but can one read four hundred pages about a literary life without reading the literature first? I decided I couldn't, and opted for the novel.

Step three: I was talking to a friend about Sally Rooney's first novel, *Conversations with Friends*, which I loved, and my friend compared it to Lehmann's *The Weather in the Streets*, one of her favorite books, she said. So then I wanted to read *The Weather in the Streets* as well as the biography, but first I had to finish *The Echoing Grove*, and then I received an email from said friend warning me that I wasn't allowed to look at *The Weather in the Streets* without buying *An Invitation to the Waltz*, a prequel of sorts, so I was stuffed: I had to read four books by and/or about the same woman. And now you're stuffed too. You have to read a column about four books by or about the same woman, a woman of whom you've probably never or barely heard. Yours is the less onerous task, but that may mean you don't read the next couple thousand words. Life is short, and there are many demands on your time. I understand.

Rosamond Lehmann was born in 1901, and if that's what I'm starting with, it looks like I'll be writing about the biography first. She wasn't born difficult, as far as one can tell, but she grew up to be a beautiful woman, and if you think that's neither here or there, then Selina Hastings would tell you different: her beauty had a profound influence on her writing, and one could argue that it wrecked her life. Glamorous men fell in love with her, but when they left her, unable to cope with her constant craving for adoration, she, too, was unable to cope. Her sense of betrayal when she was abandoned by the poet Cecil Day-Lewis (father of the actor Daniel) was such that, in 1982, she said to a friend, "There is only one person in my life I know I haven't forgiven." By this point, Day-Lewis had been dead for ten years, and he'd given her the elbow in 1950. He had been married to somebody else for the duration of his relationship with Lehmann, and she had been sexually unfaithful to him at least once (with Ian Fleming, the creator of James Bond). For a writer of such extraordinary sensitivity, she found it awfully hard to hear what she sounded like. When Day-Lewis told her he had fallen in love with someone else, she insisted that he see a psychiatrist, insanity being the only explanation she could think of for his betrayal. After the tragic early death of her beloved daughter, Sally, she became a spiritualist and spoke to Sally quite regularly; perhaps inevitably, Day-Lewis popped up from the other side to say "in a very dead voice"—well, there might be an explanation for that—"how wretched he was, and implored me to forgive him."

Lehmann's subject was love, in her life and in her fiction, and there isn't as much as there might have been of the latter, partly because there was an awful lot of the former. There were two tempestuous marriages, and a long affair with the writer, Marxist, and temporary Soviet agent Goronwy Rees, a man with the notable distinction of appearing on Google immediately if you type in the first six letters of his first name; as she got older, she contented herself with seducing her son's friends. "What's been good for the music hasn't always been so good for the life," Ben Folds sings in his song "Phone in a Pool," but of course it's very good indeed for a biography. The harder a writer works, the duller the story, by and large, and Lehmann's half dozen novels and stories over a fifty-year period leave plenty of room for fascinating and occasionally exasperating trouble.

If you like it when recognizable historical figures wander in and out of a biography, then Hastings's account of Lehmann's April of 1958 is for you: Lehmann dined with Mr. and Mrs. Stravinsky and the Huxleys at one party, and Mel Ferrer, Lauren Bacall, David O. Selznick, and Joan Fontaine at another. Her biography is good, too, if, like me, you're endlessly fascinated by the working lives of writers. There is plenty here about advances and sales, and some of the figures are startling. Lehmann's fourth novel, *The Ballad and the Source*, sold six hundred thousand copies in the US, and the film rights went for a quarter of a million dollars—*in 1945*. And yet Lehmann's career died—but it was completely reborn in the 1980s by the feminist publishing house Virago, which republished her when many of her novels had fallen out of print. It's never over.

There is also, as you might have guessed, plenty here about the peculiar domestic arrangements of early twentieth-century bohemians. We are, I would guess, much prissier by comparison, but maybe it's because we've heard about the disastrous and frankly exhausting experiments of previous generations: Cecil Day-Lewis had a two-months-on, two-months-off thing going with his wife and Rosamond, and it nearly killed him. For Day-Lewis, falling for a third party, the actress Jill Balcon—that "grotesque little piece of human material"; that "ghastly, over-emotional, fawning creature," as Lehmann wrote, with her usual staggering gall—and divorcing everyone else must have seemed like the simplest, wisest, kindest course of action.

The Echoing Grove, the novel I began with, is a good place to start, it turns out. It's not Lehmann's best book—I will announce the winner of that coveted award later—but it quickly lets you know what the author is about. There's a delicate, complicated opening chapter, a scene between two apparently long-estranged sisters, full of repressed feeling that we can't yet source, and then a flashback, sudden switches between third- and first-person narrative, lots of ellipses... We're somewhere between Austen and Woolf, but the story that emerges through the faint modernist mist is strikingly fresh and dark. The estrangement between the sisters is explained: Dinah had a passionate, anguished affair with Madeleine's husband before his sudden death. Yeah, well, that would makes Christmases awkward. It's a deeply unhappy book, written over several years and published three years after Lehmann's traumatic split from Day-Lewis; whether the author identifies with the betrayed Madeleine or the heartbroken Dinah is anyone's guess. She was certainly at home in both camps, even though she always seemed to see herself as more sinned against than sinning. I was properly converted to fandom by one phrase: Rickie, Madeleine's husband, describes the naturally contented daughter born out of his attempt to settle back into his marriage as "a laughing matter." This coinage seemed to me so simply elegant, so clever in its reversal of positive to negative, that I knew I wanted to stick around and see what else she could do.

Cynics would say that the difference between *The Weather in the Streets* and *The Echoing Grove* is easy to spot: in *The Weather in the Streets*, there is no sister, just adultery, and it's true that the two novels are not as different as they might be. Rollo Spencer, the errant husband in *Weather*, as we Lehmannites (Lehmings? Rosies?) call it, could easily be mistaken for Rickie in *The Echoing Grove*: both are charming, handsome, wealthy, not as cultured as their femmes fatales.

But then adultery is one of Lehmann's subjects, just as Rembrandt is one of Rembrandt's, and it is a pretty good one, and one not usually approached with such frankness, especially back then. And *The Weather in the Streets* contains a wonderful, chilling scene in which Rollo's powerful, privileged mother visits Olivia, the protagonist, who is sleeping with her married son, to warn her off. I can't recall ever feeling such fear while reading a novel about love and adultery. Even the ones where one of the three parties goes nuts and start stabbing people aren't as scary as Lady Spencer.

My favorite Lehmann book, though, is *An Invitation to the Waltz*, which is entirely successful in a way the others aren't, quite possibly because it's the shortest. The other two I read are baggier, and contain minor characters whom Lehmann doesn't seem to know or ever come to grips with—sinister communist doctors living in the demimonde of the East End (Lehmann was more Knightsbridge than Whitechapel; that is, more Upper West Side than Bronx) and peculiarly drawn working-class Lotharios. *Invitation* is as disciplined and single-minded as an early Nicholson Baker book; Olivia, the hapless adulteress in *Weather*, is ten years older, about to attend a dance at the Spencers', and the novel is entirely taken up with her preparations and the big night itself. It could have been a book about nothing, but it's a book about everything, or at least everything from Olivia's viewpoint. It's the beginning of the world, or the beginning of her emotional life, anyway, which is the same thing, according to Lehmann, and the jumbled intensity, the triumphs and disasters of the evening, form a superbly effective mosaic. So there we have it—that's the headline. You must read *An Invitation to the Waltz*. I'm sorry if you feel I took too long to get to that point.

Any suspicions long-term readers of this column might have had that it was artfully sculpted in some way, with literary themes elegantly educed from carefully chosen works of fiction and nonfiction, will hopefully be allayed by the inclusion of Robert Forster's *Grant and I*. What kind of idiot would end a consideration of the life and works of Rosamond Lehmann by writing about the beloved Australian indie-rock band the Go-Betweens? Well, I'm afraid there was nothing to be done. My reading is chaotic—like everybody's, I'm guessing.

The Go-Betweens meant and still mean a great deal to me. I can't explain why, but once a week or so I find myself singing a couplet from the song "The Wrong Road," from *Liberty Belle and the Black Diamond Express*, one of my favorite albums, and one of the few bright spots to illuminate the musical wasteland of the 1980s. *Grant and I* is the story of the band, which is also the story of Forster's relationship with Grant McLennan, the band's cofounder and Forster's songwriting partner, friend, burden, savior, teacher, and student. McLennan died at the age of forty-eight from a heart attack, and so, unhappily, the book describes the entirety of the relationship, in the way that *Just Kids* describes both the beginning and the end of Patti Smith's relationship with Robert Mapplethorpe. *Grant and I* is above all about being in a band that never quite made enough money or achieved enough success, even though all the music papers and everyone I knew back then loved them; unfortunately, music critics and my friends were not representative of the world at large. Forster writes really well about songwriting, touring, the fraught and fractured relationships that blight and define a collaborative life in the arts.

But this book ended up catching me by surprise in all sorts of ways. Forster is the same age as me, but in spite of living, for much of his life, on the other side of the world, his frame of reference is thrillingly similar to my own. And just as Lehmann charmed me with her "laughing matter," Forster got me with this: "[I] thought I was the smartest person at the university. Yes, really. It just didn't show up in my grades. How could it, when what I valued, a messy mix of high and low culture, wasn't being taught on campus. I knew I had something no one else had, but what?" *My university life! Described in a book! Forty years too late, but still!* Thank you, Robert. Oh, and he used to live up the road from me, and I never knew, and *Grant and I* contains a loving paragraph describing the charms of my neighborhood—my street, even. I was going to wedge this book in here whether it belonged or not. ✶

FEBRUARY/MARCH 2019

BOOKS READ:

* *Borrowed Finery*—Paula Fox
* *Making Oscar Wilde*—Michèle Mendelssohn
* *Normal People*—Sally Rooney
* *The Friend*—Sigrid Nunez

BOOKS BOUGHT:

* *Boom Town*—Sam Anderson
* *The Perfect Stranger*—P. J. Kavanagh
* *Borrowed Finery*—Paula Fox
* *What's Your Type? The Strange History of Myers-Briggs and the Birth of Personality Testing*—Merve Emre
* *Little*—Edward Carey
* *Symphony for the City of the Dead: Dmitri Shostakovich and the Siege of Leningrad*—M. T. Anderson

"**M**y father was a gambler down in Georgia," the Allman Brothers sing, "and he wound up on the wrong end of a gun. / And I was born in the back seat of a Greyhound bus, / rollin' down Highway 41." When I first heard those words as a teenager, I thought I got the gist: they were a romanticization of the outlaw spirit. Those unsympathetic to the modus operandi of 1970s Southern rock might even argue that they were unwittingly parodying this spirit, but either way, the lines were not to be taken seriously.

However, between then and now I have read enough American literary memoirs to know that the Allmans' story was almost certainly true, and almost certainly applied not just to both Allman brothers but to the rest of the band as well. Being born in the back seat of a bus before (or after) the death by shooting of a ramblin', gamblin' father, in fact, is a story that would barely hold the interest of Tobias Wolff (*This Boy's Life*), or Nick Flynn (*Another Bullshit Night in Suck City*), or Mary Karr (*The Liars' Club*), or Mikal Gilmore (*Shot in the Heart*, perhaps the most remarkable of them all). American lives, it seems to us here in the UK, are almost always enviably improbable. My own memoir, *Fever Pitch*, by sorry comparison, consists of me going to watch football matches, sometimes with my father, over four decades.

Given my insatiable appetite for improbable American literary lives, I was surprised that Paula Fox's *Borrowed Finery* had somehow passed me by. But not only is it a classic of the genre, its improbability is almost off the scale. In brief: Fox's parents, unsuccessful screenwriters whose fecklessness takes one's breath away at the beginning of the book and then builds steadily from there, put her in a Manhattan foundling home a few days after her birth, apparently because having a baby was a real drag. Her grandmother, back from a brief trip to Cuba, found out where she was and rescued her, but passed her on to a friend of the family, who in turn passed her on to a kindly preacher who lived just outside Poughkeepsie. Her mother and father reemerged and she was packed off to Hollywood—on her own, of course—where she had to deal with their drinking, and affairs, and where occasionally they both forgot to come home for the night. In other words, young Paula was still an encumbrance, so her grandmother took her to Long Island and then to Cuba. After that, things got really complicated, with stops in Florida (parents, then father, then some kind of housekeeper) and New York City and Montreal (boarding school). I have missed some steps, but she frequently seems to land in the house of someone to whom she is not related in any way.

It's a remarkable and remarkably twisty story—as twisty as anything in Dickens, including Oliver of that ilk, but it's told with a complete lack of self-pity or anger, and without judgment. The sudden leaps across the country are described with a kind of matter-of-fact, don't-ask-me shrug and extraordinary concision; the book is probably sixty thousand words long, but it could have come in at a Dickensian third of a million (*David Copperfield*, at 357,489 words, is his longest, if you must know), and the narrative alone would have justified the length. Tiny moments—the creak of an elderly knee, the hardness of porcelain when you're sleeping in a bathtub, the shrieks and moans of unhappy uncles having nightmares—carry an awful lot of the weight. It was perhaps predictable that Fox would make her name as a children's writer. She of all people knew the comfort that books could provide, and just how much comfort was needed in extreme cases. It was perhaps less predictable that she would give up her own daughter, whose father might or might not have been Marlon Brando, for adoption, or that she would later become the grandmother of Courtney Love.

I chose to read *Borrowed Finery* because I have been recommending memoirs to a friend, and I started googling to see what I might have missed or forgotten. In doing so, I also found very strong online recommendations for P. J. Kavanagh's *The Perfect Stranger*, published in 1966, a book I had never heard of, and that I have now bought but not yet read. In the previous column, I wrote at length about the brilliant Rosamond Lehmann; P. J. Kavanagh turns out to be her son-in-law, and his book is about his marriage to Lehmann's daughter, whose tragic early death pushed Lehmann toward spiritualism and effectively closed down her career. I love coincidences like this, if only because they completely justify useless hours spent fiddling around on the internet instead of working. Before I start the next paragraph, I am going to watch Arsenal's 6–1 thrashing of West Ham in 1976, now winking at me seductively from YouTube, on the grounds that I will almost certainly learn something about nineteenth-century epistolary novels.

Michèle Mendelssohn's *Making Oscar Wilde* is in its own way just as complicated as *Borrowed Finery*, and certainly covers as many miles. It's a scarcely believable but impeccably researched account of Wilde's 1882 lecture tour of the US, a trip that Mendelssohn argues gave him the tools to become the writer, wit, and chat-show fixture we know and love.

OK, so this tour… Some of you, I suspect, have been out on the road to promote a book, a film, maybe even an album, perhaps even all three. (That's how I imagine you all, as creative and glamorous and insanely successful. But you're probably just one grumpy old man who never makes anything or goes anywhere.) It's hell, right? You start out fresh and determined on Monday, and by Friday you hate people, travel, food, books, signings, and hotels, and you want to cry most of the time. Well, Wilde toured from January to August, and traveled across the entire continent of North America. He appeared in something like one hundred cities, some of which were still under construction when he got there. He spoke in Mobile, Alabama, and Brantford, Ontario, and Topeka, Kansas, and Stockton, California. True, airport security was almost nonexistent in 1882, but even so, the travel alone would have killed any of us. And he had yet to write any of the work that made his name. The reason people turned up, and what they made of him when they did, is weird, occasionally troubling, and says a lot about all sorts of things you might not have expected to pop up here, particularly race, of all things.

When Wilde was asked by D'Oyly Carte, the theatrical company behind Gilbert and Sullivan's wildly successful operettas, to talk to the American people, he was famous in London, but only as the most visible face of the aesthete movement. If you imagine that someone had somehow managed to embody the Brooklyn hipster, and then, more unlikely still, that the rest of America was desperate both to hear what the Brooklyn hipster had to say and to pay decent money to hear him say it, then you come close to Wilde's role at the beginning of the 1880s. He was parodied and mocked in London, and he'd written one play and one book of poetry, neither of which had been well received. He was in no position to turn down the offer of work. He seems to have been offered it because the longer D'Oyly Carte had a real-life aesthete out on the road, the better it could promote *Patience*, a hit Gilbert and Sullivan work that poked merciless fun at the movement.

As the tour dragged on, however, Wilde's significance changed. It was his Irishness that came to dominate, and because he was Irish, the argument seemed to go, he was more or less Black as well. At this point you could be forgiven for suspecting Mendelssohn of taking academic liberties by imposing an interpretation that rests on extremely wobbly legs, and that is suspiciously contemporary in its relevance. But the images the author provides, photographs of contemporary cartoons and advertisements portraying Oscar as an African American, or a savage, leave one in no doubt that this actually went on. "How far is it from this... to this?" asked *The Washington Post*, illustrating the question with a picture of the Wild Man of Borneo followed by a picture of Wilde. Meanwhile, Oscar spoke every night—on the English Renaissance, or "the house beautiful," or "the decorative arts," but as far as the media was concerned, he might as well have been grunting and beating his chest. It turns out to be nineteenth-century Americans, rather than Michèle Mendelssohn, who were prone to the creation of fanciful and baffling deconstructions. Meanwhile, Wilde is frequently profiled by journalists in the nascent magazine industry, and the more he's profiled, the sharper his one-liners become. They would be put to good use when he got home. I didn't know I wanted to read a whole book about Oscar Wilde, but *Making Oscar Wilde* turns out to be a book about an awful lot of things.

We praised Sally Rooney's debut novel, *Conversations with Friends*, in these pages recently. I did, anyway. I have no idea whether the Black Mountain Mob, the group of gangsters who beat *The Believer* in a card game a couple of years ago, are interested in contemporary British fiction or not, although I know which way I'd bet if they made me, as they frequently do. (Contributors now get free bets instead of a fee, which is exciting but which has been, I have to confess, unrewarding to date.) Anyway, her second book, *Normal People*, builds on the promise of the first so successfully and with such élan that if you belong to an older generation of writers and you are intimidated by the accomplishments of the young (which I am not, thankfully), then you'd want to shout, *OK, Sally. You can stop building now. Nobody will like you if you get any better than this. Plus, the thing you are building will start wobbling and fall over and some old writers will laugh.* Sally Rooney was born in 1991.

Normal People takes place over four years, but those four years constitute a significant percentage of the lives of its young characters. They're significant years that Rooney is writing about, too—the years between what you would call high school and the end of university. Connell's mother cleans for Marianne's family, and even though they go to the same school in a small town in Ireland, it's the cleaning job that pulls Connell into Marianne's orbit. Connell is a footballer, one of the boys, smart but maybe not as smart as Marianne; Marianne is a prickly loner. When they start sleeping together, Connell doesn't want anyone to know, and he takes someone else to the end-of-school dance. His betrayal of her, and his subsequent guilt and shame, sit inside their subsequent relationship like a fossil in stone. At college in Dublin, they date other people, sleepwalk into dark and frightening places, but each remains dizzyingly, confusingly bright in the imagination and soul of the other. Every page feels real. At the moment, I can't imagine not wanting to read everything Rooney writes. It will happen one day, I guess, but I know I'll devour the next one as soon as it comes out.

Earlier in the life of this column, I used to bring in details from my personal life, mostly because it seemed relevant to how and when I was reading, and, sometimes, to the kinds of things I was reading about. I had two children under the age of two when I began contributing to *The Believer*, for example, and that made a difference to my internal life. However, since roughly 2004, literally nothing has happened to me, and so I was able to focus on the books themselves. But this year, I became a dog owner, a state of affairs so profoundly shocking to me after decades of dog hating that I have yet to fully process it. If anyone had ever asked me to tell them all about myself, I'd have said, *Well, my name is Nick, and I don't like dogs, and that's all I got.* Not only am I a dog owner, but I actually like the little bastard, a cocker spaniel called George Michael (named, as you probably realized, after the Michael Cera character in *Arrested Development*, although, yes, there has been some confusion, which is irritating).

George Michael is relevant to these pages because (a) he has eaten several of the books I intended to read, and (b) Sigrid Nunez's novel *The Friend* is about a dog, among other things, and I would never have even looked at it during any other period of my life. There is even a dog on the cover, for god's sake. The narrator of *The Friend* is a cat lover who inherits a massive Great Dane after the suicide of a charismatic, much-loved friend; the dog, too, is approaching the end of its life.

And I am glad that *The Friend* and its subject matter are no longer a closed book to me. It's a lovely, sad book, full of percipient observations on the nature of grief, and friendship, and there's lots about the profession and purpose of writing; I may even be on a trajectory where I complain, in a few years' time, that there simply isn't enough dog in the book. I'm glad I'm not there yet. Right now I'm glad that George Michael has broadened my reading. I'm off to read Rilke's *Letters to a Young Poet* now, because Rilke comes up a lot in *The Friend*, so one could argue that George Michael has introduced me to Rilke. I'm sure he will make me stupid in the end, but right now he's making me smarter. ✶

APRIL/MAY 2019

BOOKS READ:

- ★ *S.T.P.: A Journey Through America with the Rolling Stones*—Robert Greenfield
- ★ *The Great British Woodstock: The Incredible Story of the Weeley Festival 1971*—Ray Clark
- ★ *Improvement*—Joan Silber
- ★ *Janesville: An American Story*—Amy Goldstein

BOOKS BOUGHT:

- ★ *The Great British Woodstock: The Incredible Story of the Weeley Festival 1971*—Ray Clark
- ★ *Fools*—Joan Silber
- ★ *The Library Book*—Susan Orlean
- ★ *Space Is the Place: The Lives and Times of Sun Ra*—John F. Szwed
- ★ *The Lost Soul of Eamonn Magee*—Paul D. Gibson
- ★ *Sevens Heaven: The Beautiful Chaos of Fiji's Olympic Dream*—Ben Ryan

In 1971 I was fourteen, and did not attend the Weeley Festival; in 1972 I was fifteen, and did not take a journey through America with the Rolling Stones, nor did I see any of their shows. Luckily, I don't have to tell you all the other things I failed to do in my teenage years, because those failures are irrelevant to my reading, and in any case I have only a couple thousand words; I am trying merely to demonstrate that it wasn't simply nostalgia that drew me to the books by Ray Clark and Robert Greenfield. I have to say, though: Those were the days, eh? I don't know why I'm asking you. You wouldn't know. You missed it all.

The Stones book may or may not have something to do with some work I may or may not be doing, but the uncertainty of the project doesn't really matter when the "research" is as much fun as this. *S.T.P.: A Journey Through America with the Rolling Stones* is a firsthand account—a kind of illustrated oral history—of a chaotic, occasionally violent, tumultuously successful tour, with as much sex and drugs as you can imagine, and then a lot more on top of that. As those who have seen *Crossfire Hurricane*, the riveting documentary about the group, will know, the Stones are probably the toughest band of them all—not tough in the sense that they would or could beat you up (Mick was and still is a skinny little thing), but in the sense that they survived situations that would have destroyed less-steely mortals. The stage invasions that ended every show in the first half of the 1960s, the death of Brian Jones, Altamont, police harassment, press intrusions... Tumultuous events flew at them like a constant blizzard of asteroids, and in 1972, crisis mode was the only mode they had known for a decade. I don't know whether you're a Beatles person or a Stones person, and the question never made any sense to me, anyway—are you a Dickens person or a Shakespeare person? But it's fair to say that the Beatles were unable to ride out the '60s in the way the Stones did.

The year 1972 was business as usual: kids battled with security guards most nights; Terry Southern nagged Keith Richards whenever he could about a movie idea; Hugh Hefner threw open the Playboy Mansion in Chicago for the weekend, and the hospitality was both abundant and exhausting; Mick and Keith were arrested in Rhode Island, already late for their show in Boston after a diverted flight, and after a photographer was punched. While the mayor of Boston negotiated to have them released, support act Stevie Wonder played for hours to an increasingly restive crowd. It's hard to read this book without feeling panicky, strung out, paranoid, and desperate, but reading books is not like singing, drumming, or moving amps was during those few weeks. The small touches of human kindness—personal assistant Jo Bergman produced a daily newsletter full of cheery chitchat—would have made me weep like a baby.

I bought Ray Clark's book after a conversation with a friend about those who feel compelled to boo art, and he remembered that Marc Bolan's band T. Rex was booed at the Weeley Festival. And because I sit at a computer all day, I immediately thought, as you do, Weeley! I remember that happening! Where is Weeley? Why was there a festival there? Why was there never another one? All of these questions seemed important and demanded immediate responses, and the next paragraph of yet another novel could wait. And the answers were sufficiently surprising for me to want to read more about it.

In 1970, the members of the Clacton Round Table, a British equivalent of your Lions Club, decided they had had enough of donkey derbies, and agreed to put on something more ambitious for their 1971 charity fundraiser—a rock concert. They were given the use of a farmer's field in the nearby village of Weeley—halfway between Colchester and Clacton-on-Sea, if that helps you to orient yourself. The original idea was to book a young, local band called Mustard to play, hopefully for a couple hundred kids, if the weather held up. But someone knew someone with contacts in the rock industry, and he set about booking some better-known names. Were King Crimson available? It turned out they were. What about Status Quo? Check. Rory Gallagher? Yep. Mott the Hoople? T. Rex? *Rod Stewart and the fucking Faces?* All good. The organizers were told to expect ten thousand people, and then fifty thousand; in the end, one hundred and fifty thousand people came.

And there was, predictably, chaos, the vast majority of it good-natured. Some people started showing up two or three weeks before the event. Those who had failed to bring camping equipment made igloos out of post-harvest straw that was lying around everywhere, and then got on with their next job, cooking their dinners on open fires. This resulted in the first, but by no means the last, calls to the local emergency services. One of the heroes of this delightful book, a kind of illustrated oral history, is the local GP, Dr. Dick Farrow. He set up a medical tent at the festival and spent the weekend dealing with a vast array of situations, some of which he was used to—sunburn, intoxication—and some of which might have been new to him. It is unclear whether he gained extensive firsthand knowledge of bad acid trips, for example, in Clacton-on-Sea, which—in the 1970s, at least—was a seaside town for elderly Londoners. (One of the organizers remembers Release, the ubiquitous 1970s drug charity, dealing with bad trips by squashing cream doughnuts into the faces of the afflicted.)

I regret to say that some of the funniest descriptions in the book are also the most violent. The Hells Angels, who were as likely to offer their security services at these events in the UK as they were in the US, started to antagonize the owners of the stalls selling hot dogs and beer. Within a couple of hours, the stallholders had raised a posse consisting of hoodlums from London's then-notorious East End, who lashed out at the Angels and their bikes with spades, pickax handles, and sledgehammers. Violence is never funny, of course, unless those on the receiving end set a great deal of stock in their ability to dish it out. (Granted, there are funny bits of violence in the first *Hangover* film, which I rewatched over the holidays. In that case, the comedy comes from those on the receiving end being completely unable to dish it out. So, you know. Works either way.)

Dr. Dick Farrow was therefore called upon to deal with a whole procession of traumatic head injuries. The police, by the way, let the gangsters do their worst, then arrested the wounded Angels and threw them in the local jail. Dr. Farrow kept meticulous notes over this longest of bank holiday weekends, and they formed the basis for government advice for years to come. The Clacton Round Table didn't make a penny. The chaos came at a price.

The past two months' reading divides neatly into two halves, because the other half… Well, I don't wish to damn Messrs. Greenfield and Clark with faint praise, because I enjoyed every single page of both their books, but both *Improvement* and *Janesville*, IMHO—and, youthful editor, please check that those letters mean something, and are in the right order—are major works of contemporary literature, as good as you're going to find in your local independent bookstore at the moment. (Oh, and publishers: if you need uncomplicated quotes for the paperbacks, ones you don't have to take any words out of: "*Janesville* is a major work of literature." "*Improvement* is a major work of literature.")

Here's what bugs me about Joan Silber: How had I missed her? As regular readers of this column will know, I *delve*. I pride myself on my delving. It's not all Philip Roth and *Fifty Shades of Grey* in these pages. Maybe I don't read enough book reviews; maybe I don't believe the ones I see. I have no regrets, really, because—thanks to a shrewd editor in the UK—I know about Silber now, and I will catch up. But there have been dry, unsatisfying periods over the last few years, when I've been itching to find fiction as good as this, and it makes me wonder what else is passing me by. If the rest of life is anything to go by, I would guess quite a lot.

First of all, a caveat. *Improvement* isn't really a novel, even though it says it is on the cover of my copy. It's a book of interlinked stories. And, yes, stories can be a tough sell to those who want to get lost in three or four hundred pages of storytelling, but Silber's way of linking is so surprising and liberating that one ends up wondering why most novels plod on with the same narrative. The first story involves a petty crime: a group of young men are buying cigarettes cheap in Virginia and selling them in New York City. One of them particularly enjoys the trips south, because he has fallen in love with a local girl. She's mentioned only in passing, and we don't get to meet her, but the next story in the sequence is all about her. The main character in the third story comes from the first, too, but we're not even aware of his existence, despite his profound significance, until he takes center stage. Once you cotton to Silber's way of working, you start to try and spot the doors she's leaving open along the way: are we going to follow this, that, her, him? She can zip backward and forward in time; she can take you to other countries and cultures. Life is a whole mess of loose ends, and we should be grateful for Silber's apparently insatiable curiosity.

But I love her prose even more than I love her unconventional narrative approach. The first story, written in the first person, seems to me like the perfect lesson in voice, and anyone trying to write or to teach writing should read it. Reyna, the narrator, is funny, shrewd, laconic, fatalistic, something of a fuckup, and refreshingly unbookish; there isn't a single line that lets the reader down, or that allows you to suspect even for a second that this person isn't real. I'm now halfway through *Fools*, and loving it every bit as much.

You, like me, have probably read other books that promise to shed some kind of light on *where we are now and how we got here*, but *Janesville* is the sharpest, the most thorough, the most ambitious, and the most compassionate, and it tells you things you probably didn't know, as well. You knew, I'm sure, that when General Motors pulls out of a General Motors town—that is to say, a town that relies almost entirely on General Motors, not only for its jobs and its prosperity but also for its purpose—an almighty and heartbreaking mess follows. What you didn't know is what happens beat by beat, year by year, as the town attempts to piece itself back together. Who takes responsibility? What can they do? How do people make ends meet? How severe are the costs? Amy Goldstein's quite brilliant book answers all these questions, and quite a few you hadn't even thought of asking— like who looks after the teenage kids abandoned by their parents in their desperate attempts to find work elsewhere?

Joan Silber, I'm sure, would admire Goldstein's novelistic eye, her sure sense of who these people are and how they're responding; strong characters emerge, not all of whom you'll like. Wisconsin congressman Paul Ryan is a Janesville native, forcing through tax cuts while the children of his electors are given deodorant and toothpaste from an emergency school-supply cupboard stocked by donations. But then it's not as if it was the election of Trump, or the Republican Congress, that ended all hope for former autoworkers. Obama pledged to help those caught "in the storm that has hit our auto towns." His administration set up both a White House Council on Auto Communities and Workers and a new Department of Labor office tasked specifically with helping these communities recover.

But after Ed Montgomery, the man leading the council, took a job at Georgetown University three days after visiting Janesville and promising to help, he wasn't replaced for a year. And the government's own Accountability Office ended up severely criticizing both the council and the Department of Labor: *You built a whole town around an auto plant, and they closed it? Well, you'll know better next time.* It's hard to imagine why you wouldn't want to read this book. It's not about economics, or about the car industry; it's about life. And we all want to know about that, right? It's why we read. ✶

JUNE/JULY 2019

BOOKS READ:
- ⋆ [Unnameable Novel 1] (abandoned)
- ⋆ [Unnameable Novel 2] (abandoned)
- ⋆ *Little*—Edward Carey
- ⋆ *Walter Benjamin at the Dairy Queen: Reflections at Sixty and Beyond*—Larry McMurtry
- ⋆ *Fools*—Joan Silber
- ⋆ *The Library Book*—Susan Orlean
- ⋆ *The Friend*—Sigrid Nunez
- ⋆ *Grant and I: Inside and Outside the Go-Betweens*—Robert Forster

BOOKS BOUGHT:
- ⋆ *News of the World*—Paulette Jiles
- ⋆ *How to Read Water: Clues and Patterns from Puddles to the Sea*—Tristan Gooley
- ⋆ *The Quest for Queen Mary*—James Pope-Hennessy
- ⋆ *Fierce Attachments*—Vivian Gornick

The first column I ever wrote for *The Believer*, over fifteen years ago, provoked a mild rebuke from the then editors. I had made a little joke about a sentence in a novel I'd read, a sentence I had decided was infelicitous, and it was pointed out to me that the magazine was a snark-free zone. I was and remain a supporter of that policy, and, a little embarrassed, I removed the joke before publication. That tiny contretemps changed my reading life forever, and for my own good. I realized the novel I'd poked fun at was not a novel I'd expected to like, particularly; I had picked it up because everyone else was reading it at the time, and I'd wanted to ask myself, What is all the fuss about? That particular question is almost always, in my experience, followed by the answer *Nothing*, because it is rarely asked in a spirit of generosity, and from that day on I started only books that looked as though they were going to suit my tastes and needs as a reader. Of course, you can't always tell, but disposition is all, and now I am always well disposed toward the contents of my fiction and nonfiction even before the first paragraph.

So what went wrong with my two abandoned novels this month? I got more than halfway through both of them, and one of them was really long, but I reached a point where I simply ran out of steam and patience, and each paragraph seemed to consist of a mix of mud and treacle. The shorter of the two was, I'm afraid, a what's-all-the-fuss-about choice, an act of recidivism that was severely punished by Tedius, the wrathful god of Boredom; the longer one was bought from a secondhand-book store some years ago as a result of the gushing quotes on the front and back covers, but proved to be, underneath its corpulence, a much leaner work than I'd anticipated, one that had let itself go. Is one allowed to fat-shame a novel? I don't suppose so. But I'm not going to post a photograph of it on Instagram, and I'm not going to name any names, so hopefully I'll get away with it. Why give books up? Why not plough on until the bitter end? Because, young friends, we want to do everything we can to break the link between literature and grim duty. You wouldn't stick with a long Spotify playlist consisting of music that displeases you; you wouldn't wade through a Netflix series you were hating. Do reading a favor and treat it as if it were just like everything else you enjoy. You're doing it in your leisure time. You don't have enough of that.

Edward Carey's *Little*, which I began shortly after giving up on the twin disappointments, was, now that I look back, a big risk for me, mostly because it's a freely imagined novel about the history of Marie Grosholtz, who would eventually become Madame Tussaud. And Madame Tussauds, the famous waxwork museum in London, is a tourist attraction that brings my city into disrepute. I pass it quite often, and there is always a long queue of foreign visitors, and I fear that once they get inside and realize they have paid good money to see pointless, life-size replicas of Benedict Cumberbatch and Posh Spice, they will hate my country and all who dwell therein, me and my family included, forever. (In one of today's cheaper newspapers—like, literally, *today's paper*—there is a photograph of Lucas Torreira, one of my team, Arsenal's, successes this season, doing Usain Bolt's signature pose alongside a waxwork Usain Bolt. If he ends up hating me and my family, we're in trouble. He's irreplaceable.) Anyway, none of this matters, because *Little* is brilliant—horrifying, unique, savage, funny, sad, beautiful, and ambitious. Edward Carey had the extraordinary vision to see that this material could, if played right, enable him to write about everything that matters: love, death, war, class, ambition, politics, money.

As far as one can tell, *Little* uses history as a base and flies off every now and again, not in search of adventure—Grosholtz lived through the French Revolution, when she was frequently called upon to cast recently decapitated heads—but in search of a rich, heartbreaking interior life. She was held in slavery by her landlady; fell in love with her son; was sent to Versailles to be the plaything of Princess Elisabeth, with whom she also fell in love; was imprisoned, prepared for execution, and freed. Some of these things may be true, and many of them are apparently taken from Tussaud's own memoir, much of which cannot be corroborated, and some of them Carey invents, gloriously. Google "Jacques Beauvisage," the thuggish young vagrant that Marie and her household adopted and apparently tamed before he went off to do the revolution's dirty work, and you will be led only to the novel; google "Benjamin Franklin and Tussaud," by contrast, and you will find that Franklin probably did know Marie. *Little* is the novel Dickens might have written if he had seen the films of Tim Burton (and had ever come to understand women). It's even been illustrated, rather wonderfully, by the author himself, rather than by Phiz, the guy Dickens used. Tedius didn't raise his head for a single page.

I wrote about my newfound devotion to Joan Silber in my last column, and I read *Fools* because I was pretty sure she wasn't going to let me down. She didn't. *Fools*, like *Improvement*, consists of cunningly, surprisingly interlinked short stories, which in this case wind their way through the last American century—in particular, the last one hundred years of belief, commitment, monogamy, integrity, all the things that complicate our lives and take us out of ourselves. The first story, the one that gives the collection its title, is about the lives and loves of a group of anarchists in 1920s New York, and the last is about a former investment banker and clubber now raising funds for lepers. "You don't know what you're going to be faithful to in the world, do you?" asks the narrator of "Two Opinions" plaintively, and Silber's characters illustrate this unpredictability with a whole range of dilemmas, all of them carefully and intricately imagined. Silber, I can tell, is never going to let me down, and I will keep a copy of one of her books, one I haven't yet read, on a special emergency get-out-of-book-jail-free shelf.

Finally, two books about books, and therefore two books about much, much more than books: Susan Orlean's *The Library Book* and Larry McMurtry's *Walter Benjamin at the Dairy Queen*. To say that McMurtry's memoir is about his relationship with literature is to risk having you skip on to the next paragraph or page: *Yeah, yeah. A writer has a relationship with literature. Big deal.* But McMurtry, author of *The Last Picture Show* and *Lonesome Dove*, probably the best book I have read in the last decade, grew up in Texas, and not in Houston or Austin, either. He lived in Archer County, ranching country, almost uninhabited when his grandparents arrived there in the late nineteenth century; fewer than ten thousand people live there now. One of McMurtry's neighbors when he was a boy was a woman who had been traded for pelts when she was a young girl, and who, when the author knew her, no longer spoke. *Walter Benjamin at the Dairy Queen* is an elegant, wise, moving account of how he read his way toward Europe, a place so densely populated that writers "could no more escape culture than I could escape geography." It's a particularly rich book for an Englishman of my age and interests, I think, as I have spent much of my cultural life trying to head the other way—toward accessibility, excitement, vulgarity, the demotic, and away from snobbery, fustiness, and deadening Bloomsbury intellectualism. And yet I still think of McMurtry as a kindred spirit, to me and to everyone who has gotten this far into a magazine dedicated to the arts, and a column dedicated to reading. *Walter Benjamin at the Dairy Queen* will take you two or three hours to read, and some of its aperçus and stories may remain with you forever.

Perhaps wisely, given the suggestion carried in her book's title, Susan Orlean's publishers have created a gorgeous, seductive object, and you'll be on your way out of the bookstore before it even crosses your mind that you could have borrowed *The Library Book*. It has an embossed red cover that gleams in the sun, no dust jacket, and it comes equipped with a facsimile of an old-school slip tucked into its cardboard wallet. It's a book I'm very happy to own, and a book I'm even happier to have read.

The Library Book is, at its core, a history of the Los Angeles Central Library. And if that sounds boring, then you have clearly never read anything else about that extraordinary city. The history of the LA Central Library is as colorful, bewildering, and quite frequently as insane as the history of Hollywood. Orlean takes as her starting point the 1986 fire that destroyed four hundred thousand books, reached a temperature of 2,500 degrees Fahrenheit, and raged for seven hours. (Orlean wonders how she missed the news of the fire. Even though she was living in New York City at the time, she found it hard to believe that a literary tragedy of this magnitude would have escaped her notice. A quick trawl through contemporary newspapers explained her oblivion: the big story that week was another fire, at a Soviet nuclear plant in Chernobyl.)

Orlean provides a gripping account of the fire and its aftermath—a seven-year period, with profound psychological implications for grief-stricken staff members, a fundraising drive, and an arson investigation. (Arsonists, it turns out, frequently target libraries.) But she also burns a book to see what it feels like, provides a brief history of book-burning both ancient and modern, and tells the story of Ray Bradbury's *Fahrenheit 451*. There is also some startling but depressingly believable information about Hollywood's use of the library: researchers used to chuck books out of the window to colleagues waiting outside, simply because they knew they'd be needing the books for a long time and didn't want to pay the fines.

If you are determined to write a library-based motion picture, there are three or four ideas in here. I'd probably start with the Great Library War of 1905, when Mary Jones was asked to leave her post as city librarian on the grounds that she was a woman. The women of LA didn't take this lying down, and there were protests; Jones, meanwhile, just carried on as if nothing had happened until she realized that her cause was hopeless. She was replaced, had already been replaced, by Charles Fletcher Lummis, an adventurer and eccentric who walked to LA from Ohio, and who published poems printed on translucent slivers of bark. His extramarital conquests were rumored to include Kate Douglas Wiggin, the author of *Rebecca of Sunnybrook Farm*, and evangelist Aimee Semple McPherson. His wife discovered a diary listing fifty such liaisons, thus scotching the theory that it was easier to keep adultery secret in the pre-electronic era. He was fired, in the end, for a great variety of infractions. Disgruntled, he pointed out that he had gone "to the roots of that Sissy Library and made it, within two years… a He-Library." I think it's fair to say that he would not have come to grips with the twenty-first century.

And, meanwhile, I keep buying books—about water, and Queen Mary, and all sorts. I don't suppose I'll read all of them, but I like to think I might, one day. Larry McMurtry and Susan Orlean and their books about books have left me with an appetite for anything and everything, just when I feared I was losing the taste. I can't wait to start whatever it is I'm reading next, and finishing it, and starting the book after that. And so on, and on. ✳

OCTOBER/NOVEMBER 2019

BOOKS READ:

* ★ *Fierce Attachments*—Vivian Gornick
* ★ *Boom Town: The Fantastical Saga of Oklahoma City, Its Chaotic Founding, Its Apocalyptic Weather, Its Purloined Basketball Team, and the Dream of Becoming a World-Class Metropolis*—Sam Anderson
* ★ *Symphony for the City of the Dead: Dmitri Shostakovich and the Siege of Leningrad*—M. T. Anderson
* ★ *On Chapel Sands: My Mother and Other Missing Persons* (published in the US as *Five Days Gone: The Mystery of My Mother's Disappearance as a Child*)—Laura Cumming

BOOKS BOUGHT:

* ★ *The Noise of Time*—Julian Barnes
* ★ *A History of the Bible: The Story of the World's Most Influential Book*—John Barton

It has been a couple of years since the Black Mountain Mob, the Las Vegas outfit who won this magazine during a card game, took over from the previous owners, the sweet-natured but naive Polysyllabic Spree. Comparisons are invidious, and it would be unwise to make them; some things (the quality of the toilet paper, for example) are better, and some things are worse: the days when visitors were offered a forty-page herbal tea menu and a dance interpretation of an Old Norse poem are long gone. But in the old days there was a dear old man called Spencer (first name) who worked, assiduously and for very little money, as the in-house historian and statistician. I understand. *The Believer* is a business now, like Google or Philip Morris, and there is no "need" for Spencer, or for Helge the masseur, or Mia the human rhyming dictionary. Cuts had to be made; I can see that.

I didn't use Spencer's services very often, but right now I miss him. I would like to know whether, in any of the fifteen-odd years I have been writing this column, I have ever had a reading month like this one. And he would have been able to tell me immediately. Spencer used to make me assign marks out of twenty-five to each book I read, a figure only ever intended for staff edification, but interesting to flick through when you had nothing better to do. Those stats have disappeared, along with Spencer himself—shot to pieces during a night of drunken target practice. (The stats, not Spencer. I don't know where Spencer went—probably to *The New Yorker*.) I actually visited Spencer's office last time I was in Believer Towers. It was occupied by a young woman called Chelseee La Rouge, who told me she was a special friend of the editor. She seemed nice, but was uninterested in the rich history of this magazine.

Anyway, by my estimate, this is a one-hundred-point column: every book listed in the "Books Read" column is, in its own way, a classic, although all classics are classics in their own way, I guess; otherwise, they wouldn't be classics.

I will begin with the oldest book here, Vivian Gornick's *Fierce Attachments*, a memoir published in 1987, and to explain how I came to read it, I need to introduce you to another character who lights up my *Believer* life, although this one is real. I have come to think of him as the Recommender, a mysterious figure who lives in New York City and suggests a book only when he is absolutely positive that I will love it. He has recommended precisely three books in ten years. The first was John Williams's *Stoner*, which was out of print in the UK when he told me about it; a couple of years later, it won the Waterstones Book of the Year award. He emails, he recommends, he vanishes, and you are left whistling softly and saying to yourself, Who *is* that guy? I suppose, like Mary Poppins, he has moved on to a reader who needs him more.

Fierce Attachments is an extraordinary, scalding book, with a fraught, bitter, verbally violent, frighteningly truthful mother-daughter relationship running right down its spine. This relationship is lifelong; *Fierce Attachments* is not a memoir that deals with a particular, defining passage of life. "My relationship with my mother is not good"—note the use of the present tense in a work of nonfiction—"and as our lives accumulate it often seems to worsen…. My mother's way of 'dealing' with the bad times is to accuse me loudly and publicly of the truth. Whenever she sees me, she says, 'You hate me. I know you hate me.'" And when Vivian Gornick tells you that something is "the truth," you don't doubt it.

Vivian grew up in the Bronx in the 1930s and 1940s with a lot of other Jewish women—there were men around, of course, but this is not about them—in an atmosphere bubbling, boiling with romantic frustration, poverty, sexual disappointment, judgment, grief, political fury. Everything was felt and felt deeply; feeling gurgled through the tenements like lava. If you are someone who feels mystified and envious whenever you go on Instagram on Mother's Day or Father's Day and see emotional tributes to a parent, this is the book for you. There are millions of us who feel completely fucked over by our parents. Millions of *you*, I should say. By *your* parents. Not all of mine are dead, although none of the survivors are *Believer* subscribers. If for some reason you are uninterested in the barbaric and unhappy blood ties that strangle us all, then perhaps you might be interested in community, women, sex, bad marriages, bereavement, or the airlessness of unhappy affairs between men and women. If you're not, I think you might have got lost. The sports results are at the back of the magazine, and the Dow Jones is about two-thirds of the way through.

There is a neat and perhaps not entirely helpful gender divide between the four books I read this month. The two memoirs, both by women, are about the authors' mothers; the two books by men are about wars; basketball; sonic booms; wild, unsettled territory. In a desperate attempt to curry favor with women readers, however, I will try not to ghettoize the memoirs. If I follow through thematically, I would be effectively saying, *Right, we're done with the mother-daughter memoirs. Let's get on with the big stuff.* Whereas actually the big stuff is always at home, right? That's where lives are shaped and shaken. Oh, don't worry. I know I'm not woke. But I like to think I've set my alarm clock, at least.

Boom Town was another tip, by another recommender. He's a good one, too, but he hasn't been at it as long as the original recommender, and I don't get the same sense that he's lying in wait, rejecting book after book until he gets a clear shot. The other guy is batting three for three, though, so he needs watching. Sam Anderson's book is about, of all things, the history of Oklahoma City, and it's a joy: funny, eccentric, brilliantly written, full of endlessly interesting anecdotes that you want to read out loud to friends. He describes the place as "one of the great weirdo cities of the world, as strange, in its own way, as Venice or Dubai or Versailles or Pyongyang."

Oklahoma City was born on April 22, 1889. Like, literally. April 22 was not the day when someone decided that a town was a city, nor was it the day when something happened that defined the city. It was not born in some metaphorical way. At noon on that day, nobody lived there. By the late afternoon, it was home to tens of thousands of people. Previously unassigned land, it was made available to all-comers by a symbolic gunshot. The all-comers had gathered at the nearest points they could, and after the shot they rode like hell to stake out their land. At 2 p.m. the first train arrived. By the next morning, there was really no space left to claim. In fact, there was no room for streets, parks, alleys, or squares, so some of these settlers had to be unsettled, much to their chagrin.

Anderson's book spans only one year in the life of Oklahoma City, but the structure enables him to tell every story worth telling about the place and its heroes: Clara Luper, a badass civil rights activist; Wayne Coyne of the Flaming Lips; basketball player James Harden; meteorologist extraordinaire Gary England, the first weatherman to think properly about tornadoes.

This is how crazy Oklahoma City is. When Boeing wanted to know what repeated sonic booms did to a city, during its development of supersonic jet travel, Oklahoma City *volunteered*. In 1964, the citizens of the city were hit with seven sonic booms a day. Children in schools were knocked out when lamps fell from the ceiling onto their heads. Houses shook. Plaster crumbled. People complained and were told by their elected representatives that they were missing out on the opportunity to prove that Oklahoma City was a city of tomorrow. The flights were allowed to continue. In the end, the city was assaulted 1,253 times over six months ("Annoyance increased steadily over the six-month period," the official report observed), and eventually supersonic flights over the US were banned. Oklahoma City's tragic desperation to please was all for nothing. I loved this book so much that I am seriously thinking about moving there.

M. T. Anderson (no relation to Sam) is a writer whose career one cannot help but follow with some astonishment. He is, in theory, at least, a children's author, but I am only just brainy enough to understand him now; I'm not sure I would have coped with his books when I was in my forties, let alone when I was a teen. His novel *Feed* is a dystopian classic, and his two-volume *The Astonishing Life of Octavian Nothing, Traitor to the Nation* is a dizzyingly ambitious trip through revolutionary Boston. I had somehow missed *Symphony for the City of the Dead*, but of course Anderson would want to write a nonfiction book for young adults about the creation of Shostakovich's Seventh Symphony. Who wouldn't?

And it's quite brilliant—moving, shocking, surprising, informative, and deeply sympathetic. Shostakovich wrote the symphony during the Siege of Leningrad, a time when both of the words for "cannibalism" in Russian, *trupoyedstvo* ("corpse-eating") and *lyudoyedstvo* ("person-eating"), were required: person-eaters were those who actually killed someone for food. In the middle of this siege, with people dying of starvation as they walked along the street, Shostakovich produced a piece of work that came to embody the Russian resistance to Hitler and was used to persuade the Americans to provide military and humanitarian assistance. The Seventh Symphony was performed by starving musicians in freezing venues; the score was smuggled out on microfilm so the rest of the world could be moved by it. You like books about why art matters? It's hard to think of an example of art mattering more than it did in that place, at that time. This being the Soviet Union, the story has a heartbreaking ending: in 1948, Shostakovich's music was banned in the USSR, and he lost all his teaching positions.

Full disclosure: Laura Cumming used to employ me to write for the literary pages of magazines, a long time ago, when I was unemployable. I owe her some kind words about *On Chapel Sands*, right? OK then. This is an incredible, and incredibly unusual, book about family, secrets, the ruinous sexual shame and hypocrisy of the first half of the English twentieth century. It's one of the best memoirs I have ever read, just as *Fierce Attachments* is one of the best memoirs I've ever read. It's beautiful, breathtakingly intelligent, and gripping. If you think I've overdone it, it's because *On Chapel Sands* is actually an incredible and incredibly unusual book, et cetera, and so on. In fact, I can't really repay my debt, because it's too fucking good. She doesn't need my help.

On Chapel Sands unrolls from an extraordinary piece of family history. In 1929, when Cumming's mother, Betty Elston, was three years old, she disappeared while she was playing on the beach of her tiny Lincolnshire village, for three days. She was found in a house twelve miles away; nothing bad had happened to her. But the disappearance was a chapter in a complicated story, one that didn't make complete sense to Betty or to her daughter for decades.

A detective story, then. Well, yes, that, too, but there is so much else. Laura Cumming, daughter of two artists, is an art critic, so *On Chapel Sands* is also about looking: looking at paintings that serve as prompts, or metaphors, or approximate descriptions (a Ravilious kettle as a metaphor for a 1930s kitchen, a Rembrandt that contains an effective depiction of the low, flat Lincolnshire landscape); looking at photographs that, it turns out, contain missed clues and buried family truths. The central incident, the kidnapping, folds out, and out, and out again, until it covers generations. It's quite brilliantly done.

If books can be opposites, then *On Chapel Sands* is the opposite of *Fierce Attachments*, because Cumming's book is about the deep, liberating, stimulating love between a mother and her like-minded daughter. Just about every page will make you envious of Laura's relationship with Betty, presuming you have or had the normal, Gornick-style parental battle zone. There is so much about *On Chapel Sands* that moves; there is so much about it that educates. It is, and will remain—like all the books described in this issue's column—a favorite, to be re-read one day, to be recommended to anyone who will listen. ✷

DECEMBER 2019/JANUARY 2020

BOOKS READ:

- ★ *Rin Tin Tin: The Life and the Legend*—Susan Orlean
- ★ *Duke: A Life of Duke Ellington*—Terry Teachout
- ★ *Elvis in Vegas: How the King Reinvented the Las Vegas Show*—Richard Zoglin
- ★ *The Dutch House*—Ann Patchett

BOOKS BOUGHT:

- ★ *Modernists and Mavericks: Bacon, Freud, Hockney and the London Painters*—Martin Gayford
- ★ *This Is Not Propaganda: Adventures in the War Against Reality*—Peter Pomerantsev
- ★ *Everything I Know About Love*—Dolly Alderton
- ★ *Siege: Trump Under Fire*—Michael Wolff
- ★ *How Democracy Ends*—David Runciman
- ★ *Run*—Ann Patchett

Where would you like me to begin? Fiction or nonfiction? Nonfiction about the golden era of big-band jazz, or nonfiction about movie dogs? I need a toe-tapper to kick off, but I have no idea which of these books will produce the desired effect. I'm guessing that, paradoxically, neither of the books about music will do the trick. If I start banging on about 1930s dance bands or Vegas-era Elvis, I'll lose you. You'll wander off to read about something more fashionable elsewhere in the magazine—Himalayan fiction, say, or sculptures made out of Juul cartridges. I don't believe I can go too far wrong with dogs. Lots of people like dogs. I'm going to start with *Rin Tin Tin*.

Having read Susan Orlean's surprising, gripping, and informative *The Library Book* recently, I found myself wondering why I haven't read every word she's written. I then realized that her previous book was about a dog, and lots of people don't like dogs. Perhaps as many people dislike dogs as like them, so maybe I was wrong to start with a book about them. At the time Orlean published *Rin Tin Tin*, I didn't like dogs much, either, so I didn't read the book, even though I bought it, but now I own a dog, through no fault of my own, and I can see they're not irredeemably terrible. Owning a dog did not make me want to read a book about Rin Tin Tin. But owning a dog did enable me to see that this was a book by Susan Orlean, one of my favorite writers; the name on the cover became more important than the jacket image or the title. Thus emboldened, I picked *Rin Tin Tin* off my shelves and immediately became lost in the sad, complicated, occasionally hilarious, occasionally baffling story Orlean excavates.

A man called Lee Duncan found the original Rin Tin Tin, or Rinty, as his close personal friends called him (and, yes, we call him that still, because he exists still, in the way that Lynyrd Skynyrd exists still), in war-torn France at the end of World War I. Improbably, Duncan got him home to the US and trained him, with apparently extraordinary success, before coming to the conclusion that Rinty was so gifted that he deserved a career in the nascent film industry. Many things were different at the beginning of the twentieth century. The idea of keeping an animal as a pet, in the house, was a new one; nobody called their dog Rover (nobody does now, either, but for different reasons); and people loved to go to the cinema to watch animals starring in movies. When Rin Tin Tin became a star, he was the *lead*, and was reviewed as an actor; the poet Carl Sandburg, then a film reviewer, said that Rinty was "phenomenal," "thrillingly intelligent," "one of the leading pantomimists of the screen." He was also paid eight times as much as his human costars.

Rin Tin Tin died in 1932, and Duncan replaced him with Junior, and then with Rin Tin Tin III. During World War II, people were asked to donate their pets to the war effort, and thousands were trained by the army. Some of them were parachuted behind enemy lines by the Army Air Corps. (A boxer dog named Jeff, an official account states with an apparently straight face, "made thirteen jumps, twelve successfully.") Rin Tin Tin III led the recruitment drive. In the 1950s, Rinty IV achieved nationwide success again, this time as the costar of a TV series, *The Adventures of Rin Tin Tin*, and by this point Orlean's book has become a brilliant if eccentric study of twentieth-century American mass media. When *The Adventures of Rin Tin Tin* goes the same way as Rinty's movie career, Orlean finds another, equally rich subject: the obsession, self-delusion, and lunacy of those on the fringes of the entertainment industry. Bert Leonard, the producer of the TV series, never let go of the idea that Rin Tin Tin had something to say to American audiences; he believed this until the day he died, in the early twenty-first century. His conviction burned so bright that he was drawn into an insane lawsuit against a woman called Daphne, who had registered ten Rin Tin Tin trademarks because she owned dogs with an authentic Rinty bloodline. The papers were served to Daphne in 1994 at a Hollywood Collectors and Celebrity Show that she had been lured to by Lee Aaker, the former child star who played Rusty in the TV series—the real Lee Aaker, not the fake one (real name Paul Klein), who for reasons best known to himself went around signing Rinty memorabilia and even spoke at a cast member's funeral. Man, there are some stories in this book. I loved every word, and it deepened my devotion to Susan Orlean's work. She is indefatigable, funny, and sees resonance and meaning in the most unlikely material. Do you need to like dogs to love *Rin Tin Tin*? Emphatically: no.

Do you need to like Duke Ellington or big-band jazz to enjoy Terry Teachout's *Duke*? I'm rather afraid you do. I couldn't in all conscience make much of an argument that the book is about anything else. Duke Ellington arrived late in my life, even later than my appreciation for jazz—I was somewhat deterred by his determination to write "suites," a tendency that suggests a craving for high-culture approval. The straight-ahead jazz came earlier in his career, and then one has to deal with the scratchiness of the recordings and the limitations of the 78 rpm form: nothing longer than three minutes. I had found enough good stuff to make me want to pick up a meaty biography, but I hadn't expected all the good things it introduced me to, nor had I expected my suspicions about the suites to receive Teachout's scholarly confirmation: Ellington always wanted to be taken seriously as a composer, but his lack of formal compositional training and the commercial imperative to write quickly and copiously meant that the suites never quite worked.

The most consistently brilliant stuff came between 1940 and 1942, when bassist Jimmy Blanton (who died of TB in '42, at age twenty-three) and the superlative tenor saxophonist Ben Webster joined what is now known as the Blanton-Webster Band. The resulting recordings are intoxicating, and my happiest cultural moment of the summer came when I listened to Ellington's "Ko-Ko" while reading Teachout's description of it at the same time. "'Ko-Ko,'" says the author, "is something else again, a relentless procession of musical events that contain not a wasted gesture. Every bar surges inexorably toward the final catastrophe, after which no response is possible but awed silence." One of the things I love about Teachout's writing is that, while it rests on a bed of meticulous research, unshowy authority, and deep musical understanding, every now and again he allows himself a couple of felicitous phrases that convey just how thrilling this music can be. The Blanton-Webster Band was a "murderer's row of soloists." About the band's performance at the Newport Jazz Festival in 1956, which raised Ellington from the dead and turned him into a *Time* magazine cover star, Teachout says: "No other rhythm section, not even Count Basie's crack team of musical arsonists, had ever played with such unquenchable fire." And the story of that Newport performance is a firecracker too. Just a year before, Ellington had a dismal two-month stint at an ice show in Flushing Meadows, and he looked to be on the way out. Newport offered a chance of redemption, but the show began limply— "the playing was sloppy, the audience response tepid." It closed with the promoter attempting to stop the show because he feared a riot, such was the hysterical response of the crowd. Teachout does the regular biographical stuff well too—Ellington was a complicated, difficult man, as his wives, mistresses, and colleagues would have told you. Richard Zoglin's *Elvis in Vegas* covers much of the same period, and contains a fascinating account of the history of Las Vegas and the entertainment the city provided ever since people started losing money there. Much of the talent came right out of the very top drawer—Sinatra and the Rat Pack, of course, but also Streisand (who bombed), Woody Allen, Judy Garland, Peggy Lee, Bob Newhart, Ella Fitzgerald, Count Basie, even Noël Coward. The money was sensational. When Sinatra left the Sands for Caesars Palace in 1967—after the infamous argument with Sands casino boss Carl Cohen, which left the singer short a couple of front teeth—he was offered (and took, understandably) one hundred thousand dollars a week. A hundred grand a week! In 1967! Other, less stellar acts had to work hard for their dough. Louis Prima and Keely Smith, who became known simply as the Wildest because of the electrifying nature of their live performances, played five times a night between midnight and 5 a.m. Everywhere, there was money being made, lost, and laundered. When Howard Hughes was asked to vacate his suite at the Desert Inn in 1966 because he wasn't spending anything at the tables, he bought the hotel instead, before buying the Sands, the Castaways, the Silver Slipper, and the unfinished Landmark. He was stopped by antitrust laws from owning 20 percent of every major piece of property in Vegas.

Elvis's first Vegas appearance was in 1956, and it went badly. The music was too raw, the show too unsophisticated. He didn't go back until 1969, by which time Vegas entertainment was struggling for relevance—none of the bands or singer-songwriters were interested in playing there, and the old guard was looking jaded and tacky. Elvis was struggling too. He made terrible movies, released only terrible songs from the movies, and his fans had lost interest in all of it. (He had no top-ten hits between 1964 and '69.) In 1956, Elvis played with his three-piece band; in 1969, he expanded to a five-piece. Oh, and a group of backing vocalists, the Sweet Inspirations, and also a gospel group, the Imperials. And, just to be on the safe side, a forty-piece orchestra. The shows were a tumultuous success. You know what became of Elvis; you know what became of Las Vegas too. Richard Zoglin's book is a clever, thoughtful, and enormously entertaining book about the good and the bad they brought to each other.

Over the summer, I listened to a friend bemoaning the absence of old-school colossi from contemporary literature: Where, he wondered, are the Roths, the Updikes, the Bellowses, the Amises (or Amiseses, if you want to include both Kingsley and Martin)? Well, right at the moment, it's true, there are no Philips or Johns or Sauls. There are, however, a ton of Elizabeths and Margarets, Anns and Megs. I fear that my friend, like a lot of men of his generation, is not a great consumer of fiction written by women, in which case he wouldn't know that actually, these days, it's all colossae, not colossi.

Ann Patchett is one of them, and *The Dutch House* is appropriately magnificent. One of the extraordinary things about Patchett's work is that she disappears inside her stories, and this lack of literary ego may be one of the reasons that people who lament the passing of the "grand old men" wouldn't necessarily notice her. You cannot predict what one of her books will be about, nor even what it might feel like—they are startlingly discrete. You know they will be smart, and true, and that they will be full of people who have been brilliantly imagined, and that when you come to the end you will feel as though you have been somewhere. But beyond that, her literary humility makes it difficult to talk about her body of work. She reminds me of my friend and occasional colleague Stephen Frears, the film director: you can try and talk about what *The Queen* has in common with *My Beautiful Laundrette* or *Dangerous Liaisons* or *The Grifters*, but I doubt you'll make much sense.

The Dutch House is a kind of multigenerational family saga, with the eponymous house at its center; I was lucky enough to read it on holiday, where it was allowed to absorb me for hour after hour, with only the occasional break for the usual exotic floor shows, elephant rides, and elaborate cocktails. My sister was with me on this holiday, as she has been on many before, and the central relationship in the novel is between a brother and a sister, over decades, so there was that too. But the protagonists, Maeve and Danny, are, like the author, buried deep in the narrative, much too involved in the complications of their own lives to worry about where theirs might intersect with yours. *The Dutch House* offers the kind of satisfaction and consolation that, I think, people look for in fiction and don't find often enough: the sense that the defining moments in the lives of ordinary people are worth describing and contemplating. Having begun with a dog, I'll end there. Susan Orlean and Ann Patchett, *Rin Tin Tin* and *The Dutch House*... If I had to live off a diet consisting of books like these for the rest of my life, I'd be running literary marathons when I was 120 years old. ✶

JUNE/JULY 2020

EBOOKS READ:

- *Life Isn't Everything: Mike Nichols, as Remembered by 150 of His Closest Friends*—Ash Carter and Sam Kashner
- *Olive, Again*—Elizabeth Strout
- *Sounds Like "Titanic": A Memoir*—Jessica Chiccehitto Hindman
- *Furious Hours: Murder, Fraud, and the Last Trial of Harper Lee*—Casey Cep

BOOKS BOUGHT:

- *Go Ahead in the Rain: Notes to a Tribe Called Quest*—Hanif Abdurraqib
- *Girl, Woman, Other*—Bernardine Evaristo
- *What Blest Genius? The Jubilee That Made Shakespeare*—Andrew McConnell Stott
- *Louisa May Alcott: The Woman Behind "Little Women"*—Harriet Reisen
- *Time Is Tight: My Life, Note by Note*—Booker T. Jones
- *Sounds Like "Titanic"*—Jessica Chiccehitto Hindman
- *Furious Hours: Murder, Fraud, and the Last Trial of Harper Lee*—Casey Cep
- *Life Isn't Everything: Mike Nichols, as Remembered by 150 of His Closest Friends*—Ash Carter and Sam Kashner

People who work in the arts have a habit of comparing themselves to other people. *How old was she when she wrote her first book? How many prizes has he won? They paid her how much? Why did they ask him to do that?* In many ways, it's the whole point of doing something creative. We feel bad—needy and damaged and hopeless—before we start a project, which is why we start it. And then, if we are lucky enough to turn our talents into some kind of job, we need to find ways of staying unhappy, jealous, and bitter. Well, do I have something for you. The new oral history of Mike Nichols, *Life Isn't Everything*, will destroy you, if the capacity for destruction is what you're looking for in a book.

Nichols—Mikhail Igor Peschkowsky—escaped from Germany and arrived in the USA with his brother, Robert, in May 1939; Robert was three, Mike was seven, and they traveled alone by boat. Nichols had alopecia totalis universalis, which meant he had no hair anywhere on his body, and his father didn't want him to own a hairpiece. He didn't get one until 1944, after his father died, leaving his family penniless. When Nichols was older, eyebrows and hairpieces had to be carefully pasted on, with a glue that by all accounts stank to high heaven. Only people of a certain disposition would, with those disadvantages, then decide to try their hand at improv, but Nichols was of that disposition, and he tried his hand and, with Elaine May, eventually created an act that was both beloved and influential. So he should have stopped there, right? I'm not saying he should have given up work. I'm not denying he had the right to feed himself. I'm saying he should have settled on a career in improv, or comedy. But no. A Broadway producer decided that Nichols could probably direct plays, so he offered him Neil Simon's *Barefoot in the Park*, and Nichols cast Robert Redford—who had never done comedy, hadn't done much of anything, really—in 1963, and the play was an enormous success. And then Neil Simon wanted him to direct *The Odd Couple* on Broadway, and that was an enormous success too. *So he should have stopped there! He should have been a theater director who used to do improv and maybe would again someday!*

But after his shows with Elaine May, Nichols used to go out to the back alley behind the theater for a drink and a smoke, and playing next door at the Majestic was *Camelot*, starring Richard Burton and Julie Andrews. So Nichols was drinking in the alley with Burton, and one thing led to another, and he directed the movie version of

Who's Afraid of Virginia Woolf? It was nominated in every single category at the Oscars, one of only two films to have been recognized in that way. All four members of the cast got nominations, and the two actresses won awards. After that came *The Graduate*, which won him an Oscar. He had already won, with May, a Grammy for Best Comedy Album, so, together with his four Emmys and eight Tonys, Nichols is one of only fifteen people in history to have won all four, the all-but-impossible EGOT.

There comes a point in any career when the white heat cools a little, and Nichols's career was no exception. His sleepy second half produced only *Spamalot, Angels in America, Working Girl, Primary Colors*, and a production of *Death of a Salesman* starring Philip Seymour Hoffman and Andrew Garfield. (Tonys galore, of course.) If someone wanted to argue that nobody in the history of the entertainment industry has a better résumé, I wouldn't know whom to put up against him. The people whose voices are heard in this book tell their own story: Paul Simon, Art Garfunkel, Cynthia Nixon, Tom Stoppard, Marsha Mason, Dustin Hoffman, Robert Redford, Steve Martin, Bob Newhart, Robin Williams, Arthur Penn, Meryl Streep, Al Pacino, Emma Thompson... And the book is a joy, as you probably could have predicted: full of sharp insights and funny stories, and with a firm grasp of narrative, not easy to accomplish in the oral biography form. I spoke to Mike Nichols twice, both times on the phone, both times about projects that either collapsed or ended up with a different director. I am telling you this not to show off, but because these phone calls were proper career highlights for me: *I just spoke to Mike Nichols on the phone!* They don't come up in this book, needless to say. Ash Carter and Sam Kashner had other people to talk to—people who actually worked with him, and knew him—about movies that actually happened.

Another person you should probably avoid reading is Elizabeth Strout, if you're of the comparative disposition. Strout has won a Pulitzer, and her books sell well, but what makes her uniquely enviable is that she has achieved a lot of this success by writing about a frequently unlikable character in a series of interlinked short stories. To say that agents and publishers advise against attempting this is like saying that, on balance, parents would prefer their children not to smoke crack. Short stories don't sell. Nobody wants to read about an unlikable character. But, kids, listen: the crack-smoking analogy falls apart at this point. There isn't an Olive Kitteridge version of crack smoking, one where the crack smoker triumphs against all odds. Yes, crack smokers can triumph against all odds, but they invariably have to do it by giving up the crack. Elizabeth Strout wrote *Olive Kitteridge*, a collection of stories with a grumpy old woman mostly at their centers but occasionally right on the edge of the frame. She won the Pulitzer, the book was adapted into a really terrific miniseries (prime-time Emmys galore), and then *she went back to the pipe*. *Olive, Again* is the result, and is every bit as smart, tender, and unblinking as its predecessor.

While reading *Olive, Again*, I found myself reminded more than once of Francis Spufford's book *Unapologetic: Why, Despite Everything, Christianity Can Still Make Surprising Emotional Sense*, in which a very, very brainy man (Spufford) tells us why he believes in God. I have no idea whether Elizabeth Strout is a Christian, and certainly there is very little religion, if any, in her Olive books. But the author's gaze, full of wisdom, pity, and understanding, is not unlike the gaze of God as described in *Unapologetic*. Here's Spufford on human frailty, a.k.a. sin:

> Taking the things people do wrong seriously is part of taking them seriously. It's part of letting their actions have weight. It's part of letting their actions be actions rather than just indifferent shopping choices; of letting their lives tell a life-story, with consequences, and losses, and gains, rather than just being a flurry of events. It's part of letting them be real enough to be worth loving, rather than just attractive or glamorous or pretty or charismatic or cool.

That, I think, is what Strout does: she takes the things that people do wrong seriously, and loves her characters anyway, and the losses and gains—especially the losses—in Olive Kitteridge's life are properly consequential. Some of these losses are inevitable and unavoidable: people die. Others, however, are a result of carelessness, or incapacity, or stubbornness, faults of character that, Strout suggests, are every bit as ungovernable as the awful stuff we have no power over. In one of the most piercing stories, "Motherless Child," Strout takes the simplest of narrative ideas—a semi-estranged son visiting his family—and turns it into something so richly imagined and emotionally devastating that when the last line comes, you feel like you've seen *King Lear* at a matinee and decided to stay for the evening performance. People are always arguing about what literature is, without ever coming up with a definitive answer. But Strout's ability to find complexity and deep, deep meaning in lives that many writers wouldn't even notice surely puts her right in the middle of the debate.

It is a relief to turn to a life in the arts that is not so enviable. Jessica Chiccehitto Hindman's *Sounds Like "Titanic"* is a memoir, the story of her career as a violinist—but before you jump to the conclusion that Hindman's life was unenviable because she had to practice a lot and she got sore fingers and the conductor shouted at her and blah, blah, I should tell you that she was what can be described only as a *fake* violinist. (And she got sore fingers and sore arms anyway.) You probably had no idea (nor did I) that there was a living to be made by pretending to play the violin, and Hindman was taken by surprise too. She applied for a job that she saw advertised on the internet—"Seeking violinists and flute players to perform in award-winning ensemble"— and got it, no questions asked, no auditions demanded, either. It turned out that the job involved touring the country and acting as though she and her new colleagues were performing the works of someone she only ever refers to as "The Composer," a man who writes the kind of easy-listening mock-classical music you can buy from a shopping channel late at night. Hindman set up a stall in a mall, turned on the CD player, and made all the right moves and even the right sounds on her violin, while a curious and charmed public handed over money for the recordings. Every single piece of music sounded like the score for that DiCaprio–Kate Winslet movie, hence the book's title; every track features a penny whistle. (You can find the identity of The Composer very quickly by googling. For the purposes of research, I spent nearly forty seconds listening to a two-hour YouTube video of his work.)

Hindman recognizes the metaphorical value of her experience, and *Sounds Like "Titanic"* turns out to be a book about all sorts of things: class and taste, for example, in another approach to the territory Carl Wilson covered in his brilliant little meditation on Celine Dion, *Let's Talk About Love: Why Other People Have Such Bad Taste* (perhaps an appropriate chime, given Celine Dion's contribution to the soundtrack of *Titanic*); the artist's insane hunger for recognition and validation; post-9/11 America and the country's need for consolation and ersatz normality. Hindman teaches writing now. It's hard to imagine a wiser, wryer guide to lead aspirants through the vicissitudes and cruelties of the life they may choose for themselves.

I suppose Harper Lee did what Mike Nichols might have done if he hadn't been so foolishly ambitious: she quit while she was ahead. *Furious Hours* is in part about a book she never wrote, a nonfiction account (very much in the style of *In Cold Blood*, by her friend Truman Capote) of a multiple-murder mystery in Alabama, Lee's home state. The Reverend Willie Maxwell was an extraordinarily fortunate man: he kept taking out life insurance on people, some of whom he was only tangentially related to, and every time he did so, that person happened to die. His first wife was found in her car on a stretch of road near her home, apparently beaten to death; his second wife was also found in her car, apparently the victim of a fatal accident. His brother was also found by the side of the road, perhaps because of a heart attack. His nephew James Hicks was found dead in a car on the road, although there were no signs of injury. Like every doting uncle, Maxwell had taken out life insurance on Hicks too. Shirley Ann, the daughter adopted during his third marriage, was found, refreshingly, *under*— rather than in—a car that had apparently fallen on her while she was attempting to change a wheel. Willie Maxwell just went on claiming the life insurance, despite the law's best efforts to prosecute him; there was never any evidence of wrongdoing. He stopped collecting money only when a distant relative of Shirley Ann's shot and killed him at Shirley Ann's funeral. Tom Radney was the lawyer who had represented Willie Maxwell during his many legal battles against the insurance companies (the insurance companies were a little unsettled by the frequency of their payouts and had begun to wonder whether anything fishy was going on). Radney got Maxwell his money; once Maxwell was dead, he got Maxwell's murderer off on an insanity plea.

You can see why this case might have appealed to Harper Lee. She studied it and the thousands of documents and transcriptions it had thrown up, perhaps for several years, and befriended Radney, but she was never able to find the book that surely lay inside the story somewhere. Casey Cep's book is gripping, blackly comic, and thoughtful, and you come away from it knowing more things than you could possibly know what to do with about the history of voodoo, the American insurance industry, and the strange, sad career of Harper Lee. *Furious Hours* is a gem.

I don't want anyone to stop, really. I want Casey Cep and Jessica Chiccehitto Hindman, neither of whom had written books before, to take the Mike Nichols path through life rather than the Lee route. I hope they write tons more books, and that these books become brilliant Oscar-winning films, with fantastic soundtracks (none of which feature a penny whistle). We need as much good stuff as people can make. I never want to stop consuming it, that's for sure. ✷

FEBRUARY/MARCH 2021

BOOKS READ:

* ★ *Nothing to See Here*—Kevin Wilson
* ★ *The Fortnight in September*—R. C. Sherriff
* ★ *Diane Arbus: Portrait of a Photographer*—Arthur Lubow
* ★ *The Art of Rivalry: Four Friendships, Betrayals, and Breakthroughs in Modern Art*—Sebastian Smee

BOOKS BOUGHT:

* ★ *The Big Goodbye: "Chinatown" and the Last Years of Hollywood*—Sam Wasson
* ★ *Ninth Street Women: Lee Krasner, Elaine de Kooning, Grace Hartigan, Joan Mitchell, and Helen Frankenthaler: Five Painters and the Movement That Changed Modern Art*—Mary Gabriel
* ★ *How to Do Nothing: Resisting the Attention Economy*—Jenny Odell
* ★ *Nothing to See Here*—Kevin Wilson
* ★ *Selected Writings of Gertrude Stein*—Gertrude Stein
* ★ *English Journey*—J. B. Priestley

Do you remember the pandemic? I ask because I have to submit this column a couple of months before publication, and I am imagining that we will be through it and out the other side by the time you get to read it. Or maybe you'll pick up this issue of *The Believer* in a couple of years, and you'll be like, *A pandemic?* And you'll have to put the magazine down and consult Wikipedia to remind yourself of what went on in 2020. I am joking, of course. Normally I wouldn't say, "I am joking, of course," but that feeble effort is the first joke I have made since March, and I have lost my moorings. You've probably lost yours too.

You might have hoped that this column could provide some respite from the troubles of the world, but our consumption of books has been profoundly affected by them. Some of us have found reading hard; some of us have read more, including *War and Peace* and *Ulysses*; some of us have avoided dystopic or otherwise miserable fiction while wolfing down endless Agatha Christie novels; some of us have started more than seven thousand books, only to find that not a single one of them is speaking to us in ways we can hear. My best and easiest reading time was over the summer, when it looked like everything was returning to normal. Now winter is approaching, and in Britain, at least, the virus is back and looking more menacing than it did in the spring, and once again, I am trawling my shelves for *le livre juste*, without having a clue what that book should be about, what tone it should have, how many pages it should be, whether the words should rhyme, what language it should be in. Let's avoid the present, now and for the foreseeable future, when talking about books or any other subject, and I will take you back to my sunny garden and the few weeks when literature made perfect sense.

Kevin Wilson's *Nothing to See Here* is a novel about class and friendship, and it has a lot to say on both these subjects. Madison Roberts and Lillian Breaker meet at an exclusive prep school for girls. Madison is beautiful, and has money, and is now married to a senator; Lillian was a scholarship girl from a single-parent family but got chucked out for possession of cocaine. The cocaine actually belonged to Madison, but Madison's father offered Lillian's mother some money to induce her to persuade Lillian to take the rap. Now Lillian is working in a supermarket, living back at home, all promise and ambition long abandoned. The novel begins with Madison reaching out in a letter and inviting Lillian to visit her in her mansion.

There are other novels like this, and one might happily read them and get all empathetic about injustice and marvel at the tenacity of friendships and so on. But here's the thing: Madison now has two stepchildren who catch fire, spontaneously, when they get stressed-out, and she wants Lillian to take care of them. And that's what makes *Nothing to See Here* a work of genius: surprising, funny,

sad, and completely original. This is the second book by Wilson
I have read that contains these qualities. His first novel, *The Family
Fang*, was just as fresh, just as lovable, although perhaps the clean
lines of *Nothing to See Here* give it an edge. Either way, Wilson is
a fantastic talent, and that talent, fellow pandemic-reading strug-
glers, is honed to provide books so smart and entertaining that you
want some kind of government authority to make him write more,
quickly, and tell other writers how it's done. We need novels like
this urgently.

The only other author I know of who manages to find room
for spontaneous combustion is Dickens, in *Bleak House*, although
Dickens was sufficiently chicken to inflict the calamity on a minor
character. Bessie and Roland, Madison's stepchildren, are necessarily at the center here, because they cause a lot of trouble to all
concerned—they do no harm to themselves when they get worked
up and incendiary, but they are a danger to curtains, and their carers,
and so on. And if you're reading this and wondering how Wilson gets
away with it tonally, then imagine what, say, Anne Tyler would do
with the material: she would get in close, and observe with sympathy
and, when appropriate, humor, and you would believe immediately
that this is just another condition we don't know about, albeit one
that speaks convenient volumes about the ways in which adults can
damage their kids. I craved *Nothing to See Here*, and I had no idea of
this craving before I began it.

I'm not sure whether R. C. Sherriff's *The Fortnight in September* is a
sale that's harder to close with readers in the US, but I am going to try
anyway, because it meant just as much to me, in completely different
ways, as Kevin Wilson's novel. I came across it in one of those "What to
Read When the World Is So Fucking Awful" lists that our newspapers
were full of a few months ago; most of the suggestions seemed both
useless and actively cruel to me, but Kazuo Ishiguro recommended a
mostly forgotten 1931 novel by a man better known as a screenwriter
and the author of the play *Journey's End*. (The play is familiar to every

British male of a certain age who went to a single-sex school, which is just about all of us over the age of sixty, because it is about the First World War and there are no women in it.) Ishiguro called it "the most uplifting, life-affirming novel I can think of right now," and I had bought it before I finished the rest of the paragraph.

The bad news first: the entire book is about the kind of British seaside holiday that might make more fortunate nationalities weep for us. Cheap foreign travel brought this kind of vacation to an end, but not before generation after generation had experienced endless rainy days in Bournemouth or Bexhill or, in this case, Bognor Regis, the shabby hotels and boardinghouses, the disastrous food, the quiet evenings spent doing crosswords or playing cribbage. We used to look forward to them too. *The Fortnight in September* documents every single moment of the Stevens family's two weeks away, early Nicholson Baker–style—they don't get off the train at Bognor Regis station until the twelfth chapter—and yet it somehow manages to be both enthralling and heartbreaking, without ever stretching the discipline or truth of the novel. There are five Stevenses—a mother, father, two grown-up kids, and a younger boy—and each of them is granted a moment of profundity, or drama, or self-recognition, and the inherently undramatic contexts for these moments make them all the more surprising and powerful. Sherriff is also quite brilliant on how annual holidays distort and accentuate the passing of time: "Today it had travelled gropingly," Mr. Stevens reflects on the first evening, "like an engine in the fog, but now, with each passing hour of the holiday, it would gather speed, and the days would flash by like little wayside stations. In a fortnight he would be sitting in this room on the last evening, thinking how the first night of the holiday seemed like yesterday—full of regrets at wasted time." As someone who has spent every one of the last eleven summers with the same families, and has gone from worrying about the children drowning to worrying about the children drowning while drunk, I found something especially meaningful in *The Fortnight in September* and its melancholy, angular intimations of mortality. These two novels are among my favorites ever, the books I will recommend to friends for as long as I have a memory, or friends. What a miracle that I should come across both in the bleakest of years.

Books about art, or at least about artists, seemed to hit a spot, too, and only partly because artists are mad and funny and live lives designed for the prurient enjoyment of those who come after them. It was news to me, for example (although probably not to you, dear sophisticated *Believer* reader), that according to Arthur Lubow's long, exemplary, and authoritative biography, Diane Arbus maintained a sexual relationship with her brother throughout her life. It's the little things like that which hook you in, but you stay hooked because of the description and dissection of Arbus's art: I can honestly say that this is the first time I have properly understood how and why photography has the right to be considered a true expression of self in the way that writing and painting are. There is an extraordinary story here about the picture *Woman on a Park Bench on a Sunny Day*, a rather mournful portrait of a middle-aged woman wearing a sleeveless dress, her face etched with troubles but trying out a smile anyway. A friend of Arbus's, on seeing the picture, reacted with shock for two reasons. The first was that he had seen the woman many times, and she had always seemed happy. Those who don't like Arbus's work would feel that the choice of print confirms the photographer's dark worldview, that her thumb was always on the scales. But the second reason for the friend's reaction was that he knew that the woman on the park bench had committed suicide not long after the shot was taken. Arbus took her own life, too, of course, so what did she see in the woman on the bench? The little boy in the photo *The Child with a Toy Hand Grenade in Central Park, NYC* grew up to be someone who recognized himself in the picture only when he was older and wiser. Of the photo, he said, "She saw in me the frustration, the anger at my surroundings, the kid wanting to explode but can't because he's constrained by his background… She's sad about me. 'What's going to happen to him?' What I feel is that she likes me. She can't take me under her wing but she can give me a whirl." As Lubow says piercingly, "She was a dowsing rod for anguish."

Sebastian Smee's *The Art of Rivalry: Four Friendships, Betrayals, and Breakthroughs in Modern Art* is every bit as grounded in the real and the biographical as the Arbus book, even though it is, in essence, a work of art criticism, and works of art criticism can, at their worst, float away from what you can see and learn from pictures way off toward the clouds, and you find yourself thinking, Well, what if I don't feel that? What if I'm not disoriented, or made uneasy by the shock of the new, or discomfited by the gaze of the sitter? But Sebastian Smee is way too good a writer to rest anything on the vague and the hopeful, and the four relationships in his book were all intimate, real, tumultuous, and deeply significant in the careers of the artists concerned.

Here's how unfanciful, how substantial and demonstrative, these relationships are: A drunken hug between de Kooning and Pollock resulted in Pollock falling heavily, pulling his friend down on top of him. Pollock broke his ankle. After Pollock's death, de Kooning took up with Ruth Kligman, Pollock's lover and the sole survivor of the car crash that killed him. The portrait that Degas painted of Manet and his wife, currently in an obscure museum in an industrial city in Japan, is now incomplete—Manet cut part of it away, perhaps as a response to what he felt it revealed about his marriage. This book is biography as criticism, and it is, I think, spectacularly successful.

But that was then; this is now. As I write, London is heading back into partial lockdown. Starting tomorrow, we can no longer visit our friends in their homes, or meet them in restaurants or pubs. Winter is approaching, and the light and hope of the summer are disappearing. We must again retreat into our heads. This isn't a test of the power of the written word, of novels and memoirs and poetry. The written word has seen off every challenge that the world has thrown at it since the invention of the printing press. But it is a test of our relationship with books, of how well we know what we want from them. Looking around, I see I have started Ben Folds's autobiography; Elizabeth Jane Howard's novel *Getting It Right*; Phyllis Rose's *Parallel Lives: Five Victorian Marriages*; Ann Wroe's book about Pontius Pilate... Something will hit the spot, and if it doesn't, I will keep looking. I have to. ✶

APRIL/MAY 2021

It is impossible to write about the music of 2020 without writing about the music of 1970, right? You just have to. Well, not *you*, maybe. But I am a man of a certain age, and if anyone releases any music in a year that ends with a naught, then men of a certain age feel a moral obligation to compare that music to the music released in other years that end in a naught. That's just the way life is. And if you can go back a pleasingly round fifty years to compare, then the imperative is even more pressing. It's more or less the law. A half century! I'd been waiting for 2020 to arrive since 1989. That it arrived in a state of some disarray, raging and plague-ridden, is of no concern to us here. People still made recorded music. If they didn't want to be judged against history, then they should have worked harder and got their stuff out in 2019. Or worked less hard and gone for 2021. But no: they had the hubris to risk the zero.

So let's begin by looking at the albums of 1970. It was the year of *Layla and Other Assorted Love Songs*, by Derek and the Dominos, and the home of one of my favorite-ever guitar solos, by Eric Clapton, on "Nobody Knows You When You're Down and Out." (I prefer James Burton to Clapton most of the time, but the solo here is deeply musical rather than extremely fast, and it kills me every time.) And there's the Velvet Underground's *Loaded*, the album containing "Sweet Jane" and "Who Loves the Sun" and a few other tracks I've been listening to ever since, quite often while watching a support act in a club. It was the year of the Grateful Dead's *American Beauty*, and the Stooges' *Fun House*, and the Who's *Live at Leeds*, and George Harrison's *All Things Must Pass*, and Van Morrison's *Moondance*. You may have heard one or two of the tracks on *Bridge Over Troubled Water*—the title song, for example, which begins "When you're weary, / feeling small"—and a couple more on the Beatles' *Let It Be*. My favorite Aretha album is *Spirit in the Dark*, I think, and if you haven't bothered with the nearly eleven-minute version of James Brown's "Get Up (I Feel Like Being a) Sex Machine" (on the album *Sex Machine*) until now, then what is COVID for? (I understand you might not be feeling *exactly* like being a sex machine, but see how you get on.) *Ladies of the Canyon* was a 1970 record, and *Led Zeppelin III*, and *Déjà Vu*, and *Paranoid*, and *Curtis*, the one that gave us "Move On Up," and the first Funkadelic album.

Anyway. You get the picture: lots and lots of classics, albums you have heard at least some of even if you were born in this millennium. But let me tell you, young people, how we listened to albums in the 1970s: we listened to them over and over again. I owned probably three albums in December 1970, and maybe twelve by the end of 1971, and that was all the music I had access to. Sometimes I borrowed a friend's record, and sometimes I listened to the one BBC station that played pop music, but they played mostly chart music, and I didn't like Andy Williams or Rolf Harris that much. (I will explain the phenomenon of Rolf Harris, an Australian children's entertainer, another time, but he is not long out of prison, and we should probably not stir it all up again.) The albums I owned I turned into classics through sheer force of will. If I didn't like it the first time, I played it again until I liked it more. Nobody of my age can be trusted to tell you about classic albums of the 1970s and how much better they were than anything that's come since, because we never listened as hard to anything ever again. The only two 1970 albums I owned in 1970 were *Paranoid* and *Live at Leeds*, neither of which I would sit through again. I bought most of the others in later years, as my tastes broadened and I found out more, but most of them have been cannibalized, reduced to favorite tracks on playlists.

And, let's face it, a lot of those albums are shibboleths, more often nodded at nostalgically than consumed. *All Things Must Pass* was a triple album, and a third of it consisted of musicians jamming to no real purpose in the studio. *Let It Be* is the Beatles' shoddiest record, sad aural evidence of all the discord that preceded the band's undoing. It's by the Beatles, so people forget, or never knew, that the reviews were hostile—"a cheapskate epitaph, a cardboard tombstone," said *New Musical Express* at the time. It ended up on *Rolling Stone*'s infamous white-rock "500 Greatest Albums of All Time" list anyway. Those artists all had an advantage too. The music Neil Young made on *After the Gold Rush* didn't exist even six years previously. There was a whole fresh, unexplored world out there, an unspoiled planet. In the fifty years since, artists have claimed more or less every available plot of land as their own, and younger people have had to write better, think harder, create imaginative extensions to the existing geography to get noticed.

Which brings us to 2020, a year so extraordinarily, dazzlingly full of great albums and great songs that it is entitled to feel a little sorry for the old-timer. *Really? That's the best you could do? Even though you had an unspoiled musical planet? And we had rampant disease?* To be fair, the rampant disease seems to have assisted the music-making, or at least removed the distractions and alternative (and vital) income streams that usually prevent so much music from being recorded. The year 2020 was when some people released two great albums, or one great double album; you could pick pretty much any particular genre and list ten records you may or may not end up listening to for the rest of your life. If folk-country is your thing, then you might love Sarah Jarosz's *World on the Ground*, or Jason Isbell's *Reunions*, or Lucinda Williams's *Good Souls Better Angels*, or my particular favorite, Katie Pruitt's *Expectations*, or my other particular favorite, Waxahatchee's *Saint Cloud*, or Kathleen Edwards's *Total Freedom*, Tami Neilson's *Chicka Boom!*, Chris Stapleton's *Starting Over*, Elizabeth Cook's *Aftermath*, the already deeply beloved debut *Bonny Light Horseman*. That's ten, and I'm leaving out Gillian Welch and the Drive-By Truckers, which obviously can't be done. In other words, there's a great folky-country record for every month of the year, a record that would repay close attention. But who's got the time for close attention? Even when all we've got is time? And who wants to limit themselves to folk-country? And if you do, then you'd better make some room for both *Evermore* and *Folklore*, Taylor Swift's breathtakingly good offerings this year. You can play the same game with hip-hop, and R&B, and probably manage a whole separate ten for the subgenre of artists who combine elements of both.

Here's something that happened in 2020: the Prince estate released the *Sign O' the Times* boxed set, which contains sixty-three previously unreleased tracks. That on its own is a staggering amount of new music, a collection that really demands a month of focused listening. If it had come out a year after the original album, I probably wouldn't have listened to much else that year, not least because a good chunk of my annual music budget would have been blown on the one artefact. Oh, and Tom Petty's 2020 *Wildflowers and All the Rest* nearly doubles the length of the original *Wildflowers* album, which was as perfectly realized as Prince's masterwork, if less formally ambitious. Bob Dylan released the extraordinary *Rough and Rowdy Ways* and the brilliant "Murder Most Foul," an elegy to America that sounds sadder with each passing breaking news atrocity. Springsteen released the rock-solid *Letter to You*. The song I played the most in 2020 was the Pretenders' "You Can't Hurt a Fool," a song to rank alongside the best Chrissie Hynde has ever written, and therefore a pop-rock classic. Prince, Dylan, Petty, Bruce, the Pretenders—you could have spent the entire year listening enthralled to people pushing seventy, pushing eighty, no longer with us. I have forgotten the great new albums by Swamp Dogg (age seventy-eight), Bettye LaVette (seventy-four), and Toots Hibbert (who died this year, at age seventy-seven)—they belong in this paragraph too. The Rolling Stones have managed only a terrific zeitgeist number one single.

I haven't even mentioned the music I admired the most last year. Phoebe Bridgers has yet to release a song that hasn't caused my heart to stop, at least for a moment, and sometimes for worryingly longer than that, but that might just be an unconnected age thing. I suppose she'll make music I don't like someday, but there's no sign of it happening soon. *Punisher*, her second album, is perfectly crafted, perfectly sad, even when it's poppy and riffy. The song "Kyoto" begins, "Day off in Kyoto. / Got bored at the temple. / Looked around at the 7-Eleven," and you think, Come on, Phoebe, you can't be writing about rock-tour ennui already. And within no time at all, a few lines, she's getting into some kind of painful family thing clearly involving the narrator's father. (Interviews with Bridgers will lead you to the conclusion that, in this case, the narrator and the singer cannot be separated.) "And you wrote me a letter, but I don't have to read it," she sings in the second verse; "I'm gonna kill you if you don't beat me to it," she sings in the third. The ache in the voice and the song is something I haven't come across before, despite the familiarity of the setting, like she's trying to find as much consolation as she can amid the sore spots. If you want to see how deep she can cut when she wants to, check out "Funeral" from *Stranger in the Alps* ("Jesus Christ, I'm so blue all the time," runs the lovely chorus) or her devastating version of Tom Waits's "Georgia Lee." Twenty-one million people have listened to "Kyoto" on Spotify at the time of this writing, a number I find deeply comforting. She's a big deal, and an old soul.

Nobody knows that much about Sault. They made two rapturously received albums in 2019, and two more, *Untitled (Black Is)* and *Untitled (Rise)*, in 2020. Their Wikipedia page is four lines long. They are British, some of them, but one of the prominent singing voices belongs to an American, Melissa Young, known as Kid Sister. The songs were written by UK producer Inflo and Cleopatra Nikolic, better known as Cleo Sol, whose album *Rose in the Dark* also came out in 2020. These people are on a scalding creative streak. What do Sault sound like? A lot of things—Portishead, sometimes, or Soul II Soul, or Fela Kuti—but everything sounds great, and "Wildfires" is an instant classic.

Did I listen to too much music in 2020? Emphatically, no. I wish I'd listened to more. It was, as you probably know, a tricky year, and music never fails to provide solace, inspiration, cheer, excitement. Is it possible to listen to too much *new* music? I rather fear it might be, and I don't know what to do about it. I have referred to a lot of artists in this piece, and a lot of new albums, and even now I'm remembering things I've loved over the last few months (HAIM! Maria Schneider's *Data Lords!*) that didn't fit into the entirely arbitrary categories I've made here. But my relationship with it is of necessity shallow, or certainly not as deep as the relationships I made with records fifty years ago. Those were the days in which the fade-out of one song immediately enabled me to anticipate the intro to the next, and guitar solos could be hummed note for note, even the solos on *At Fillmore East* by the Allman Brothers Band. Does that mean I have lost something? Have I swapped the depth of a marriage for the narcotic cheap thrill of a hundred one-night stands? Or has the constant exposure to the new simply created a different kind of listener? I would like to think three or four of these albums will be my constant companions forever, but that isn't going to happen, I suppose. Newer music will come along, and then there's all the old music; maybe those of us who have listened to new music all our lives have different ears now that we all own everything. ✶

JUNE/JULY 2021

BOOKS READ:

* *On the Cusp: Days of '62*—David Kynaston
* *Minor Characters: A Beat Memoir*—Joyce Johnson
* *My Rock 'n' Roll Friend*—Tracey Thorn
* *Secrets of Happiness*—Joan Silber

BOOKS BOUGHT:

* *Albert and the Whale: Albrecht Dürer and How Art Imagines Our World*—Philip Hoare
* *Light Perpetual*—Francis Spufford
* *Mike Nichols: A Life*—Mark Harris
* *Suppose a Sentence*—Brian Dillon
* *A Swim in the Pond in the Rain: In Which Four Russians Give a Master Class on Writing, Reading, and Life*—George Saunders
* *Cary Grant: A Brilliant Disguise*—Scott Eyman

I have said it before, probably irritatingly, and I will say it again several more times: one of the most remarkable literary projects of this century is being undertaken right now, as we speak, by the social historian David Kynaston. Since 2007 he has been publishing a series of books about Britain between the years 1945 and 1979, when Margaret Thatcher came to power. There have been three so far: *Austerity Britain: 1945–51, Family Britain: 1951–57,* and *Modernity Britain: 1957–62*—roughly 2,300 pages, or 135 pages per year. If you are going to treat a country as a person, full of personality, development, joy, tragedy, regression, and contradictions—and that is what Kynaston does—then an allocation of 135 per year is actually pretty disciplined. (If, in the year 2070, someone embarks on a similar project, then the year 2020 will demand several hundred thousand words of its own.) These wonderful books deal with politics and town planning, sport and literature, music and movies, cities and the countryside, and a rather gripping narrative somehow emerges, in the same way that improvising jazz soloists find melodies.

Anyway, luckily for me, Kynaston has decided that 1962 deserves more than its fair share of attention, and the result is *On the Cusp*. What were we on the cusp of? The most obvious answer to that question is that the 1960s, or what we later came to think of as the 1960s, were about to be born—and not all over the world, but in England, of all places. The Beatles released their first single; a band called the Rollin' Stones (no *g*, and, for the moment, no Charlie Watts or Bill Wyman) played their first show.

But in the meantime, this is what our radio sounded like, a description provided by an unhappy contributor to the letters page of *Melody Maker*, who had been confined to his sickbed: "After three minutes, I turned off Sandy MacPherson. The Metropolitan Police Band sounded like the British police. Left with 'The Dales' [a genteel radio soap opera], Scottish dance music and the BBC Midland Light Orchestra, I picked up my book again." There was nothing else in Britain for young people at the time. We had two TV channels, both broadcasting in black and white; you couldn't buy a drink after eleven o'clock; hardly anyone had central heating; many people had an outside toilet and electricity provided by coin-operated meters. If you had gone to your bookmaker in 1962 to ask for the odds on this dark, wet, grumpy country becoming the center of the pop-culture universe within three years, you might have decided to put your money on something more likely, such as Mister Ed becoming the first talking-horse president of the US.

But there were other things about to happen, apart from the Beatles and Mary Quant. The liberal left was on the rise, and there were signs that the influence of the old, reflexively snobbish Britain was beginning to fade. (A ludicrously posh cricket correspondent—*yes, we even had posh sports writers*—was once described as "so snobbish that he wouldn't travel with his own chauffeur.") And, incredibly, with the country just beginning to think about joining the Common Market, later the EU, there was another way of dividing up the country: into those who believed that our future lay with continental Europe, and those who regarded anyone who didn't speak English with deep suspicion. In other words, we were having exactly the same fucking argument as the one that tore the country down the middle in the second decade of the twenty-first century. The big problem then, as now, was that the division was not conventionally political, and certainly could not be characterized as the conservatives versus the left. The leader of the Labour Party, Hugh Gaitskell, finally came down on the side of those who distrusted any kind of federalist project; the conservative prime minister, Harold Macmillan, was pro-European. Mollie Panter-Downes—*The New Yorker*'s London correspondent, whose clever, perceptive columns have provided Kynaston with plenty of valuable insights over the course of his sequence—thought the battle lines had been drawn thus:

> The young, by and large, appear to be in favor, with an instinctive feeling for the big new moment in history and the wider chance, and so are the businessmen, eager to get going in the great new market, plus a majority slice—one could perhaps risk guessing—of educated, thoughtful opinion. The various anti-Market meetings that have been held in different parts of the country have drawn many retired service people, maybe disturbed by the thought of a still further dwindling of the British influence that they helped, in their time, to impose around the world.

She would have written nearly exactly the same about the mood in 2016, which rather begs the question: What happened to the young? Because it was the old who voted for Brexit, and yet they were not old in 1962, if I may point out the bleedingly obvious. Perhaps what happened to the young people then is what always happens to young people. How many in the US, one wonders, voted for Carter *and* Trump? That's the great thing about great books. There's always something in them that makes you want to hang yourself, whatever they're purportedly about.

Five years before the Beatles released their first single, Jack Kerouac published *On the Road*, although he had written it quite a long time before that, in April 1951. I don't think I had quite understood this fact before reading Joyce Johnson's lovely memoir, *Minor Characters*, and it made me look at the book slightly differently. I had always understood it to be of the moment, but I now see it was of quite another moment altogether. Kerouac's first novel, *The Town and the City*, came out in 1950; there followed seven long years of writing and traveling and bumming around, and many of the books that saw the light of day (*The Subterraneans*, *Doctor Sax*, *Tristessa*, *Maggie Cassidy*, as well as several posthumously published works) were written long before his overnight success. It doesn't matter, of course. *On the Road* turned out to be enormously influential, but it influenced a generation who would have been too young to dig it if it had been published a few months after Kerouac had completed it. Perhaps it came out at the perfect time. America was introduced to that bebop prose at a time when bebop had been given plenty of time to bed in: Kerouac's voice was fresh but not scary, and pointed the way toward the American 1960s, just around the corner.

Minor Characters, first published in 1983, fourteen years after Kerouac's death, is a beautiful book about the people he knew in New York. Joyce Johnson was his girlfriend of sorts, although there were others, and almost by definition he wasn't around that much, anyway. The title is wry, but there is a truth to it, at least as far as Kerouac and his fellow travelers were concerned. At the beginning of her book, Johnson describes the fate that befell Joan Vollmer, the wife of William Burroughs. Vollmer, as you probably know, dear, smart *Believer* reader, was killed by her husband while he was playing a drunken game of William Tell with a .38. "Joan Vollmer Burroughs's death is much more famous than she is," notes Johnson, and the observation introduces us to the world she chooses to portray here, a world populated partly by admiring, overlooked, patient, and disappointed women. But Johnson was there with Jack on the night he read the life-changing review of *On the Road* in *The New York Times*, a review that would never have achieved the same effect if the crusty old fiction reviewer for the *Times* hadn't been on holiday, replaced for the week by a younger, more sympathetic critic: "We returned to the apartment to go back to sleep. Jack lay down obscure for the last time in his life. The ringing phone woke him the next morning and he was famous." *Minor Characters* is about a lot of things—being a young woman in the 1950s, bohemia, art, fame, friendship—and I have to say I had a better time reading it than I have ever had reading Johnson's more famous ex-boyfriend.

Here is a terrifying and shameful list. And, by the way, I'm talking about my lifetime here, not this month:

⋆ Books I have read about Henry VIII, Queen Victoria, or any British king or queen: 0 (that I can remember)
⋆ Books I have read about the natural world, especially plants and trees: 0
⋆ Books I have read about chemistry: 0
⋆ Books I have read about computing, et cetera: 0
⋆ Books I have read about the history of just about any country: 0
⋆ Books I have read that are in part about the relationship between Lindy Morrison and Robert Forster of the Go-Betweens: 2

You don't need me to tell you this isn't good enough, really. There is a decent chance you haven't come across the Go-Betweens, an under-appreciated Australian indie-rock band, now deceased, who made records beloved by music nerds and the French. I am not French, as you might have begun to suspect, but I suppose I am a music nerd. The Go-Betweens' records are beloved by me, predictably, and when Robert Forster wrote a book about his relationship with his friend and the band's cofounder, Grant McLennan, who died in 2006 at age forty-eight, I was there. One of the factors that affected the relationship between McLennan and Forster was the relationship between Forster and the drummer, Lindy Morrison, so I was already up to speed; Tracey Thorn's *My Rock 'n' Roll Friend* is about her relationship with Morrison, so we get to see the Forster-Morrison relationship from a new angle. I won't apologize for being riveted. Regular readers of this column will know I have read books about other relationships, some of which were invented by their authors, but there is something about the world of the Go-Betweens—their commitment to their music, their charm, their bad luck, the way they always seemed destined to appeal to a tiny band of devoted fans—that speaks to many parts of me. And, in any case, *My Rock 'n' Roll Friend* is about the relationship between two women, one shy and successful (Thorn was the singer in Everything but the Girl and has made several well-received solo records), the other loud and fierce. "As much as I'm drawn to her outrageousness and loudness," Thorn writes, "I'm drawn to her *positivity*. She is constantly upbeat, which is also in my nature. We are both full of a curious, almost gauche enthusiasm about the world. We are cheerer-uppers, bounce-backers, irrepressible, determined—me in a quiet way, her in a noisy way." Who wouldn't want to read a book by a cheerer-upper in times like these? And Thorn is not an unreflective cheerer-upper, either. This book is thoughtful, perceptive, occasionally raw, and eye-wateringly honest. I may have read too many books about the Go-Betweens, but there aren't too many memoirs about contemporary female friendship.

Joan Silber wasn't in the Go-Betweens—how smooth a bridge from one para to the next was *that*?—but she is one of the people I read who makes up relationships, densely complicated connections between people, as a way of thinking about the world. That's probably just a clunky way of saying she writes fiction, but her new book, *Secrets of Happiness*, like its predecessors *Fools* and *Improvement*, is a different kind of fiction. The stories are interlinked, but not interlinked in the

Olive Kitteridge sense, through one character or place. The opening story, "Ethan," is about a young man who discovers that his father has a secret family; the next, "Joe," is about one of the kids from that secret family; and the next, "Veronica," is about Joe's ex-girlfriend. Silber leaps across continents and decades, characters age and screw up and die, but the astonishing detail of her imagination keeps any of it from seeming glib. We end up back with Ethan, now a single, middle-aged man nevertheless entangled with the sister and adopted daughter of an ex-lover's deceased partner. Sometimes the dexterity and plenitude of Silber's plotting take your breath away, or make you want to laugh. Why isn't there more fiction like this? I don't mean, you know, why isn't there more fiction in which a minor character in one story becomes a major character in the next. (Although why isn't there more of that too? It's a really cool way of writing.) I mean, why isn't there more fiction that's such a pleasure to read, simply because of its clarity, wisdom, heart, and elegance? *Secrets of Happiness* feels like a benchmark, a guiding star, a minimum height requirement; I'd like to say I will never again settle for fiction that's not as good as this, but I know I will have to. ✶

OCTOBER/NOVEMBER 2021

BOOKS READ:
* *Prince and the Purple Rain Era Studio Sessions: 1983 and 1984—* Duane Tudahl
* *Last Chance Texaco: Chronicles of an American Troubadour—* Rickie Lee Jones
* *What White People Can Do Next: From Allyship to Coalition—* Emma Dabiri

BOOKS BOUGHT:
* *Wayward Lives, Beautiful Experiments: Intimate Histories of Riotous Black Girls, Troublesome Women, and Queer Radicals—* Saidiya Hartman
* *The Mere Wife—*Maria Dahvana Headley
* *Beowulf: A New Translation—*Maria Dahvana Headley
* *London War Notes: 1939–1945—*Mollie Panter-Downes
* *Prince: The Man and His Music—*Matt Thorne

66 **I** slipped through school with a B average in spite of not being able to read very well," says Rickie Lee Jones in *Last Chance Texaco*, her gripping, lovely memoir. "I could read but I could not concentrate." It's a confession one suspects crops up in a million autobiographies by people who work in entertainment. Ozzy Osbourne probably wasn't a focused reader in school, and it's hard to imagine Elvis sitting in a well-lit corner flogging himself through *The Adventures of Huckleberry Finn*. What is remarkable, however, is that this admission occurs on page 167 of a 350-page book about a life that began in the mid-1950s and a career that began in the late 1970s. I know what you're thinking. You're thinking, You must be joking. I love Rickie Lee Jones, but I'm not reading seven volumes about her. But it's not

like that. The pages leading up to her assessment of her high school career are thrilling, funny, scary, sad, packed full of life and extraordinary characters. It becomes very clear that these moments and these people are responsible for her career, her lyrics, even her sound, and you don't really need to know what mics she used, or what the record company did wrong with the promotion of the ninth album. She describes the genesis and success of her first two albums in detail and with fresh excitement, but they are the culmination of something, not the beginning.

Her grandfather was Peg Leg Jones, a vaudeville entertainer who could do a flip from a standing start, despite his eponymous disability; her mother was brought up in an orphanage; her father went off to seek his permanently elusive fortune when he was just shy of fourteen, and fought in World War II. He was sixty-three when he died—"younger than I am now but older than anyone in his family had ever been," a heartbreakingly simple description of life on the American margins. Rickie Lee's sister Janet was a handful who ended up in a home for wayward teenagers, and her brother, like her grandfather and also her uncle, lost his leg in an accident. Her mother and father fought, made up, moved, moved again. "What were they running from? Well, they ran from cities, houses, and eventually themselves, but they never got away from their difficult childhoods or their love for each other." (I wonder, by the way, what the geography of England has done to our artists? The English have bad luck and grinding poverty and explosive marriages, too, of course, but we don't have anywhere to run, really. I mean, you can keep moving and moving, but you can never move very far, and you can never escape the weather, or the architecture, or the culture. You have to move in your mind rather than in your pickup truck.) Trouble was heading for Rickie Lee. There was just too much heartbreak, poverty, chaos, and impermanence to avoid it. Rather than sit around and wait for it to arrive, Rickie Lee went out to head it off at the pass.

In 1970, she hitchhiked up to Big Sur from Long Beach, California, where her family was trying and exhausting their luck. She lived in a cave for a while with a bunch of hippies, but then she and a new friend decided to go and see Jimi Hendrix at the Ventura County Fairgrounds. Mind duly blown, she returned to the cave, only to find that the cave dwellers were moving on. They vowed to reconvene in a little town in Canada for July 4. Rickie got there, but only one of the cave crowd had bothered. She decided to travel back to the US with a guy who was crossing the border to buy pot. She was arrested and jailed, initially with adult criminals who were "howling like banshees." This happened when she was fifteen years old. All this takes up the tenth chapter of her book; it would occupy seven hundred pages of mine. Such are the terrifying twists and turns of the drama, and the immediacy and detail of the scenes, that one can occasionally be tricked into thinking one is reading a novel, and into making guesses about the eventual outcome of this young woman's life. I didn't have much hope for her celebrating her sixteenth birthday, let alone her sixtieth.

Studded throughout the book, like gleaming clues to a happy ending, are references to music, in particular the music that provided the singular jazz-folk-Broadway-rock-soul stew of her first album. She sees *West Side Story* at the movie theater as a little kid and is thunderstruck. She teaches herself Bob Dylan's "House of the Risin' Sun" and Barbra Streisand's "People" ("Musically, I was 'Barbra Dylan,' a collage of all I had heard"). She hears and is spooked by Dr. John while high during her Canadian adventure. And, perhaps most importantly, she comes across Laura Nyro, "not like anything else evolving out of the 1960s, as if the singer of the Shangri-Las had been raised by Leonard Bernstein." She had found her person, the one most creative people need to complete a metamorphosis. "Somehow, the moment I fell in love with Laura I loved myself just a little more. I believe an invisible cord came out of me and attached itself to Laura Nyro that summer. Or vice versa." As a portrait of the artist as a young woman, this book could not be any more enthralling or fun to read. Her troubles are not behind her, of course, once she has found her calling: the account of her breakup with Tom Waits, who walked away when he found out she was using heroin, is particularly piercing. You feel it, presumably because the author still does. Her first album of covers was titled *Girl at Her Volcano*, a lovely way of describing influence. But many volcanoes have the capacity to blister the skin.

I don't know what Rickie Lee Jones means to you. She means a lot to me. Those two first albums are perfect, I think, and sound even better to me now—as if they were somehow newly minted, but the ambition, the voice, the arrangements, and the songwriting seem like greater achievements, after the forty years I've spent listening to things that aren't quite as good. I was in my early twenties when I first heard them, and I thought great albums would come along every few weeks. Rickie Lee was a pretty cool role model for me too. If I am not the worst man in the world—and I can think of at least seven off the top of my head whom I'd like to think I'm better than—then she is one of the women who helped drop me down the list. Jones spends some time describing the terror and the joy of being on *Saturday Night Live*, her first TV appearance, right when her first record came out. You can watch a grainy, hissy video of it on YouTube, and I recommend you do: She's note-perfect, rocking her trademark beret, happy, apparently full of confidence, and ready to burn down the world. The band swings and the audience adores her. It's impossible not to be moved by it, once you've spent a couple hundred pages discovering how she got there. I loved this as much as I loved Dylan's *Chronicles* and Patti Smith's *Just Kids*.

What white person wouldn't want to read a book called *What White People Can Do Next*, in the current climate? I am being flippant, regretfully. Both you and I can think of a ton of white people who wouldn't want to read it and aren't going to, and even those who follow the smart young academic Emma Dabiri on Twitter became unhappy when they heard about her book. "Before the book was even written, I had 'white' people tweeting me to tell me how offensive the title is." (We'll get to the quote marks around the word *white*.) Dabiri is not, as you might have guessed, a "white" person, and although the idea that a disastrously well-meaning "white" person might have written a book called *What White People Can Do Next* is comical, it's not entirely beyond the realm of possibility, judging from some of the encounters Dabiri describes in the book. After she took part in a public discussion on Afrofuturism, the blues, trap music, and ancestral veneration, a woman approached her to express her disappointment that there had been no mention of "allyship"; in other words, what's the point of Black people if they're not prepared to talk about white liberals and their willingness to help?

There is so much in these 150 pages that I found useful. In the chapter titled "Interrogate Whiteness," Dabiri asks us to let go of the whole notion of "whiteness." White people, as she points out, are "a relatively modern invention." What does Tucker Carlson really have in common with a Caucasian man in Flint, Michigan, who hasn't worked for ten years, or with a fisherman in England whose livelihood has been destroyed by the unintended but calamitous results of Brexit? They really have very little white privilege to check. Those of you who have seen *Judas and the Black Messiah* will recall Black Panther Fred Hampton's smart, successful attempts to form a "rainbow coalition" among impoverished and aggrieved residents of all races. As the poet and cultural theorist Fred Moten said, "This shit is killing you, too." And Dabiri is withering in her critique of the tendency of well-meaning whites to slip into the white savior lane: "Black people do not need charity, benevolence or indeed guilt…. As such, allyship appeals to a desire to help a 'victim,' constituting a reification of the power imbalance." There is so much I want to quote; maybe you should just read it. If you need any further persuasion, Dabiri calls the anthropologist Margaret Mead a "Karen," and provides a toe-curlingly unreflective Mead quote to prove her point.

I separated *Last Chance Texaco* from *Prince and the Purple Rain Era Studio Sessions* because I wanted to give the impression that I am a rounded individual and not just a relentless music nerd. Fuck it, I am a rounded individual, when it comes to reading, at least, but a Rickie Lee book *and* a Prince book? Come on. What's a rounded individual supposed to do, apart from raise his hands in surrender and promise to read more nineteenth-century fiction in the near future? I would recommend *Last Chance Texaco* even if you have never heard the author's music, but I don't think Duane Tudahl would really mind if I told you that if you don't love Prince, then this isn't the book for you. Tudahl's book is a day-by-day account of Prince's work in the studio between the beginning of January 1983 and the end of December 1984, during which period he became a global superstar. There are a ton of interviews with some of the people who were there with him—band members, the long-suffering and fascinating engineer Susan Rogers (now—and you probably saw this coming—a professor, after earning a doctorate in music cognition and psychoacoustics). Prince being Prince, Stakhanovite hard work, imagination, and lubriciousness are never very far away: the recording made on December 31, 1983, and January 1, 1984 (Happy New Year, Susan Rogers!), involved both the oud and the riq, an Arabic tambourine. The song was called "We Can Fuck," and it featured the sound of Prince's friend Jill Jones in the throes of orgasm. That's a lot of the oeuvre in a nutshell.

Those of you who checked out the expanded *Purple Rain* a few years back already know that he recorded much more than he needed for the album. But he was also making albums at the same time for Vanity 6 (who were replaced by Apollonia 6), the Time, Jill Jones, Sheila E. and the Family, and occasional tracks for Sheena Easton. His creativity and output were staggering. Oh, and "making albums" means writing them, producing them, and playing most of the instruments on them. This could lead to friction, especially with the Time, who in the movie were the big-shot band that the Prince character was trying to surpass. In real life, and even though the Time was a proper band rather than a collection of Prince sock puppets, Prince took over and sacked a few of the band members who he felt were ill-disciplined. The truth, as becomes clear in Tudahl's book, is that he was more talented than everyone he played with. He was a better drummer, guitarist, keyboard player, and singer than anyone who might find themselves in the studio with him. That kind of talent is always going to spell trouble.

This isn't a gossipy book, nor does it try to decode Prince or tell us what he means. It is an attempt to discover his art through the truth of its creation, and that makes it invaluable and unique, certainly in the field of music writing, and rare in all arts writing. Tudahl intends to write books about the next few albums in this golden run, and I'll be there waiting for them.

I read a novel this month, too, a good one, and it isn't about music. It is about love and marriage and adulthood and all the things I am *just as interested in as music*. But I seem to have run out of space, and I will have to write about it next time. ✶

DECEMBER 2021/JANUARY 2022

BOOKS READ:
- ✶ *Oh William!*—Elizabeth Strout
- ✶ *Cary Grant: A Brilliant Disguise*—Scott Eyman
- ✶ *The Burgess Boys*—Elizabeth Strout
- ✶ *Wild Game: My Mother, Her Secret, and Me* —Adrienne Brodeur

BOOKS BOUGHT:
- ✶ *Wild Game: My Mother, Her Secret, and Me*—Adrienne Brodeur
- ✶ *The Burgess Boys*—Elizabeth Strout
- ✶ *Sorrow and Bliss*—Meg Mason
- ✶ *The Turning Point: 1851—A Year That Changed Dickens and the World*—Robert Douglas-Fairhurst
- ✶ *Franchise: The Golden Arches in Black America*—Marcia Chatelain

Cary Grant fell in love with Sophia Loren during the filming of the 1957 movie *The Pride and the Passion*. Grant was married at the time, to Betsy Drake; Loren was in a relationship with the Italian film producer Carlo Ponti, who was also married. Grant told the writers of another movie he was intending to star in, *Houseboat* (based on a story by Betsy Drake), that he'd found the next Garbo, and that they should rewrite their script accordingly. Disregarding his own wife and Loren's lover, Grant proposed to Loren, but she turned him down. He felt humiliated and angry. He was then appalled to discover that Loren had been cast in *Houseboat*, forgetting that this had been his request in the first place, and tried to walk out of the production, but his contract prevented him from doing so. He now hated Loren and didn't want to be around her. However, once filming started, he forgot he hated her and proceeded to fall in love with her all over again, but he was still married, and she still had a lover, so the results were the same.

Cary Grant would've been a deeply irritating fictional character—exasperating, mercurial, self-involved, psychologically implausible, and with an entirely improbable backstory. An acrobat troupe! Tumbling! Yeah, right. The weird thing about Grant, though, is that he *was* a fictional character, in the sense that he made himself up: a working-class Bristolian kid called Archie Leach, who got himself to New York as part of the aforementioned acrobat troupe and then moved from musical theater into movies. He borrowed liberally from his characters until he became "himself"—suave, sophisticated, always impeccably dressed. (He was frequently referred to by ignorant American film industry types as a "Cockney," by the way. He wasn't one. Cockneys are born within the sound of Bow Bells, in East London, and Grant was born a hundred miles from there. You're not a Cockney even if you're born in Notting Hill or Brixton. But then what does it matter to you people? As far as you're concerned, the whole of England is part of the set of *My Fair Lady*.)

If you knew nothing at all about Grant, you might guess that there was some trauma somewhere that created his impeccable surface, a surface that seems to go all the way to his core, and you'd be right. Grant's father had his mother committed to an asylum when he was eleven years old. He was told that she disappeared, then later that she was dead. Grant and his father moved in with his grandmother, but this seemed only to intensify the poverty that blighted the family, and Grant effectively ran away to join the circus when he was fifteen. He didn't find out that his mother was alive, and would have been sufficiently sane to manage life outside an institution, until his Hollywood career was underway.

Scott Eyman's biography of Grant is an absorbing, nuanced account of an elaborately constructed person who could have existed only during the exact years he lived. There aren't so many acrobat troupes these days, for a start, and it's much harder for a man to decide that his wife belongs in an institution just because it is convenient for him. But there's something about the way the world was back then, pre–World War II—when ideas of class were more rigid; secrets could remain hidden; aspiration was less complicated, and invariably involved champagne and good suits—that enabled the idea of Grant. And if you're looking for "Was he gay?" gossip, I'm afraid this is not a salacious book, although it does properly examine the rumors, most of them centered around his bachelor housemate relationship with Randolph Scott. All one can say is that anyone who married five beautiful women, and who was temporarily destroyed by his failure with Sophia Loren, was not a gay man, although he might well have been attracted to both sexes. He never seemed to mind the gossip much. He took the view that women always wanted to find out for themselves, and their curiosity worked to his advantage.

One of the melancholy pleasures to be taken from Eyman's book is its depiction of entertainment as a very straightforward business. Nobody wanted to make a movie that was unwatchably miserable, or excruciatingly slow, or repellently violent, and nobody wanted to watch one; there was either dumb fun (*The Bachelor and the Bobby-Soxer*—"Most agreeable," said *The New York Times*) or sophisticated fun (*The Philadelphia Story*, *The Awful Truth*, *North by Northwest*, et cetera). Pre-Hollywood, it was even simpler. Some of the vaudeville acts unearthed by Eyman include "The Twelve Speed Maniacs," which consisted of a dozen men who built a Model T in two minutes and drove it off the stage; "Think-a-Drink" Hoffman, who came onstage with a portable bar and a cocktail shaker and asked the audience what they wanted; and Al Lydell, "America's Foremost Portrayer of Senility." I don't know about you, but I would pay any amount of money to watch any of these people tonight. I suppose these things go in cycles, and what goes around comes around. We'll just have to wait until our hunger for pornography and art movies has been sated before we can buy tickets for a night with "Think-a-Drink." At the moment, you can't grab anyone's attention unless there's at least one genital mutilation.

Elizabeth Strout's characters are the complete opposite of Cary Grant, as real as Grant was a confection. Strout is beginning to put together a remarkable collection of books. (I guess the right way of saying "a collection of books" is "oeuvre," but, you know, we don't speak like that in these pages.) At the moment she seems to be writing two different sequences: there are two Olive Kitteridge books and three Lucy Barton books, if one includes the short-story collection *Anything Is Possible*, which is set in the town Lucy Barton grew up in. These books constitute five of the last six. The Kitteridge books are written in the third person—Strout must have realized pretty early on in her conception that Olive's flinty, grouchy exterior is best observed from the outside—but *My Name Is Lucy Barton* and the latest, *Oh William!*, are narrated in the first person. Lucy's quiet, sad wisdom, which occasionally breaks into the kind of despairing, puzzled fragments exemplified by the title, is just great, a literary marvel, and an object lesson in how to create character through voice.

My Name Is Lucy Barton is set more or less entirely in a hospital ward. Lucy Barton, a writer with a scarred, impoverished back-ground, is sick, and her mother comes to visit her, and they talk. Lucy is looking back on all this when she tells us the story, and toward the end of the book she says, "My mother was right; I had trouble in my marriage. And when my girls were nineteen and twenty years old, I left their father, and we have both remarried. There are days when I feel I love him more than I did when I was married to him, but that is an easy thing to think—we are free of each other, and yet not, and never will be." That rich little confessional moment provides the substance of *Oh William!*

William, the husband Lucy left, has remarried twice since she was sick in the hospital, and his third wife, Estelle, leaves him during the first act of this new book. Lucy's beloved second husband, mean-while, has died, and she is still mourning him. So they are both single again. Shortly before his calamity, William is given a genealogy kit as a present, and discovers he has a half sister. (Genealogy kits are not yet fictional clichés, but anecdotally I have been told about so many unwelcome discoveries that I fear they may soon become so.) He and Lucy end up going on the road to look for this sister together. This may sound very high-concept for an Elizabeth Strout novel, but fear not: plot takes up very little of the space she allows herself. This painful book is about regret and incomprehension, grief and parenthood, the apparent impossibility of self-knowledge. It's maybe the best of her wonderful books—or at least, it's the one that cuts the deepest. Over the summer I read *The Burgess Boys*, which is also terrific, but it's much closer to being a conventional novel: sharp; beautifully written, of course; elaborately plotted; its hardscrabble town and half-broken inhabitants reminiscent of *Mare of Easttown*. But the interesting thing about the Lucy Barton books is that her language is frequently artless. "So there was that as well," she says at the end of a story, where Vonnegut might have said, "So it goes." Another one begins, "But." And there is the frequently uttered cry of "Oh, William." It's an extremely effective way of conveying the pain and confusion of a writer: Lucy Barton is so watchful and precise that you just know her books wouldn't read like that. It is very rare that you read a writer at this stage of a career, nine books in, and end up knowing you will read everything she writes.

The familial complications in Adrienne Brodeur's extraordinary *Wild Game* are maddening, improbable, disastrous, ill-judged, and sometimes just plain badly constructed—all possible flaws in a novel, but dynamite in a memoir. *Wild Game*, I should add quickly, is a memoir. We don't diss novels here at *The Believer*. When Brodeur was fourteen, her mother, Malabar, woke her up to tell her that she had just been kissed by Ben Souther. Ben was the best friend of her husband, Charles, Adrienne's stepfather. Ben had a wife, too: Lily. The two couples were extremely close. Malabar was glamorous, a brilliant cook, gregarious; Ben was outdoorsy, hearty, a hunter-gatherer. Their spouses were both sick. Charles had suffered a series of strokes at the beginning of his marriage to Malabar that left him incapacitated; Lily was damaged and frail after her cancer treatment. If this were a novel, you'd end up thinking Brodeur had read too much D. H. Lawrence.

Adrienne (and perhaps we should think of the confused and vulnerable girl in the book as Adrienne and the perceptive author as Brodeur) was shocked, of course, but she quickly realized she was being asked to facilitate the adulterous relationship, to plot and hide and share in her mother's excitement, and that was what she did, for years and years and years. She was invited to share fantasies about the honeymoon that Malabar and Ben would surely have; she helped cook up the stories that would explain absences; she lied to her stepfather when corroborating alibis.

One of the themes of this book—or one of the things it makes you think about, anyway—is this: At what age do we become the person who must take responsibility for the mistakes we have made? I won't own up to anything I did before the age of seventeen or eighteen, but round about that time it starts to become a little difficult. You do dumb stuff when you're eighteen, and, yes, you are young, but you are also semi-recognizable to yourself. Adrienne was too young to understand the depths of the waters she was swimming in when she was asked to dive in, but she's still in those waters when she's at college. And she's still waving—or drowning—when she marries Jack, Ben's son, who has no idea about the affair when they get together, at which point, unsurprisingly, things start to unravel for nearly everyone. Brodeur is scrupulously fair and refuses to talk her way out of anything she might have been responsible for, but the truth is that she was injected with a microchip that night when she was fourteen, and there was nothing much she could do about it until she realized she had to tear it out of her own arm. Malabar and Ben go to Italy for their honeymoon, and Adrienne's husband becomes her stepbrother. You won't find a memoir as gripping as this one; each strange turn in the narrative makes you gasp at the madness and folly of people in love. And it's right up there with Vivian Gornick's *Fierce Attachments* in its depiction of the intensity of the mother-daughter relationship and its ability to disfigure lives. I can think of ten women off the top of my head I'd want to give this book to.

It's the end of the English summer. It rained, mostly. But these were the books that made the wet and the cold bearable. When the sun eventually did come out, and I found myself reading Elizabeth Strout on a sun lounger by a pond, the brightness and warmth seemed almost de trop. We have all learned something like that these last eighteen months: that the outside world doesn't matter so much if we allow talented people to cast their light when we need it. ✶

ABOUT THE AUTHOR

Nick Hornby is the bestselling author of eight novels, including *Just Like You*, *About a Boy*, and *High Fidelity*, and several works of nonfiction, including the memoir *Fever Pitch*. He has also written numerous award-winning screenplays for film and television, including *An Education*, *Brooklyn*, *Wild*, and, most recently, *State of the Union*.

NICK HORNBY
CONTINUES READING

★ ★ ★ ★ ★ ★ ★ ★

JOIN HIM!

★ ★ ★ ★ ★ ★ ★ ★

In addition to Nick Hornby's quarterly column, every issue of *The Believer* features a full-color comics section, original essays, and interviews that are frequently very long and almost always quite untimely. One annual special issue comes with an ever-changing bonus item, such as an art object or a free radio series. Simply fill out the form below for your special Hornbyphile discount!

Visit **thebeliever.net/subscribe** *and use code* **"ROSAMOND"** *to receive one year of* The Believer *(four issues) for a discounted rate of just $50*

· ·

Or mail in this card to get one year of The Believer *for the same rate!*

NAME: _____

STREET ADDRESS: _____

CITY: _____ STATE: _____ ZIP: _____

EMAIL: _____ PHONE: _____

CREDIT CARD #: _____

EXPIRATION DATE: _____ (VISA/MC/DISCOVER/AMEX) CVV: _____

Make check or money orders out to McSweeney's Literary Arts Fund, and mail this form to:
The Believer, 849 Valencia Street, San Francisco, CA, 94110